Design

Restart: New Systems in Graphic Design

Christian Küsters + Emily King

Thames & Hudson

Contents

NEW SYSTEMS IN GRAPHIC DESIGN

Graphic designers like systems. Why? The answer emerges from graphic design history. According to established historical accounts of the profession, graphic design flourished in the decades after the Second World War, but its success depended on servicing the prevailing cultural criticism of the period.

Graphic design had finally escaped the straightjacket of modernist formal restraint. Through the 1980s and into the 1990s, designers explored this new-found liberty to the fullest extent. The resulting spiral of excess is often considered to have culminated with the formally elaborate a head when a loose international coalition of voluble graphic designers – Katherine McCoy and April Greiman in the United States, Wolfgang Weingart in Switzerland, Gert Dumbar and Jan van Toorn in the Netherlands – began to make their presence felt. Although they had diverse concerns, they were grouped together and described as 'postmodern' to satisfy the

This rough history has been crafted by rounding the edges of a much messier tale. Setting the stage for the 1980s postmodern epiphany involves overstating the dominance of graphic modernism. Likewise, sketching the scene for postmodern disaffection requires making the theoretically impossible assertion that each and every one of the avenues suggested by postmodern theory have been exhausted (and also ignoring the fact that the large part of mainstream graphic-design practice remains untouched by these developments). Nevertheless, it is a story with which a substantial part of the graphic-design community identify. The sense of helplessness engendered by the untamed

modernist graphic design), but this is not correct. New systems in graphic design are derived from a huge variety of disciplines – mathematics, technology, science, geography, the everyday, politics, linguistics, literature, art – and their outcomes are multiple and eclectic. Through the adoption of systems, graphic designers have been able to break new conceptual ground, to go beyond formal tweaking and to move into uncharted waters of visual meaning.

The Graphic Concept
The systems of graphic design that are explored in this book represent significant new moves in visual communication. Because the featured work foregrounds idea above form, some designers and critics

recent essays on conceptual art have dwelt upon the formalist concerns of its most important protagonists. Indeed, many of the graphic designers in this book revealed a self-consciousness about form. Some suggested that the book should go entirely unillustrated, as if demonstration of how it looked would compromise discussion of what it meant. Others appeared to deny the deliberations behind carefully taken formal decisions. This seems all wrong — graphic ideas succeed because the designers behind them have a keen understanding of how form works. The illustrations in this book are an exploration of the effective use of graphic form.

Experimental Graphic Design
Conceptual or not, the work in this book is for the most part non-commercial. The greater proportion of the projects shown here are initiated by the studios themselves and those that are not are almost uniformly created for the marginal end of the graphic market, such as **cultural institutions. Mainstream audiences are often nonplussed by this kind of work, not understanding the point of graphic design if it is not being used in the service of mass communication. Designers are frequently accused of inappropriately aping the practice of fine artists, and on occasion they themselves**

commercial existence. In denying the audience an immediately gratifying image, graphic designers are retreating into a mode of work that is not so easy to consume. Of course gallery owners and art collectors caught up with conceptual artists pretty quickly – turning non-objects into commodities at the wave of a chequebook. Similarly popular visual taste catches up with image-denying graphic designers at quite a rate – in the ceaseless succession of styles, non-image becomes image in the blink of an eye. Perhaps calling any image or object conceptual makes a claim on cerebral integrity that is difficult to maintain.

Furthermore, designers cannot completely evade the issue of form. it makes

New Systems in Graphic Design

corporate machine and promoting the monolithic world view of international capitalism. The graphic style adopted by designers to encourage this view has been called modernist, and it came in Swiss and American variants – the Swiss introduced the puritanical version, while the Americans produced the easier-to-

swallow, consumer-friendly variety. Modernism in graphic design was primarily a formal system whose aim was to create seamless visual uniformity, to process disparate information into a homogeneous product.[1] Graphic modernism thrived for several decades, but by the mid-1970s it

was under threat. The certainties of international capitalism were questioned and the modernist outlook no longer seem viable. Designers around the world began to tamper with modernist orthodoxies, and in the early-1980s these transgressions came to

and commercially successful work of West Coast designer David Carson. Graphic designers may have been free, but they were not happy. What at the outset had seemed a critical challenge to the rigid mind-set of modernism had degenerated into a visual free-for-all. Design commentators began to notice a move away from the

'postmodern style' as early as 1995, when Dutch critic Carel Kuitenbrouwer wrote of a 'new sobriety' in Dutch graphic design.[2] Turning their back on free expression, graphic designers opted for restraint – and this is where the system comes in. There is nothing like a system for creating a sense of control.

mannerisms in postmodernism is very real. Designer Andrew Blauvelt asks, 'Is there no way forward when everything seems possible?'[3] A return to discredited strictures of modernism is not an option, so the system is the route by which designers can escape the formal impasse; the system is a life jacket that allows designers to bob

around on the perilous waters of graphic form.

To some, the idea of the graphic system might seem like a covert return to the self-evident verities of graphic modernism. 'System' seems to imply that there could be a singular graphic process and a definite graphic solution (a core idea of

no sense to talk of graphic design that is purely conceptual: graphic ideas are visual ideas – ideas about word and image – and form is a vital element in their execution. But it is not only image-denying graphic designers who stumble over form; object-denying conceptual artists have also tripped up here, and several

have used the term 'conceptual' to describe this kind of approach. Given that the strategies of contemporary designers do echo those of the 1960s generation of conceptual artists this is somewhat apt. These artists were often motivated by the desire to make work that was harder to buy, art that would be less compromised by its

1. See Michael Worthington essay, p. 163.

2. Kuitenbrouwer, Carel. 'The New Sobriety', Eye (vol. 5, no. 17, Summer 1995).

3. Blauvelt, Andrew. 'Complex Simplicity', Eye (vol. 9, no. 35, Spring 2000).

make claims to artist status. This results in a set of questions: is it art? Is it non-art? Is it bad art? As perplexing as these questions are, the search for answers never amounts to much. It seems most productive to view this kind of graphic design as graphic experimentation rather than pseudo-art or art by default. The term

the contents of their inner being may be an important aspect but there must be more at stake. Central concerns of any would-be graphic author are the issues of accountability and ambition, both of which touch on the points raised in the 1999 *First Things First* manifesto (a revival of Ken Garland's 1964 original). The signatories subscribed to the notion that primarily

graphic design ought to be a socially motivated activity. An admirable ambition, but its expression in *First Things First* was limiting. Obviously social good is a worthy goal, but equally obviously the singular pursuit of that goal, as it is described in the manifesto, may well prevent designers from forming an imaginative view of the factors that actually

I will be arguing that they are equally applicable within disciplines such as architecture, fashion, product design or fine art.

Spirit Not Letter
Restart is not meant to offer an agenda to graphic designers – I am not trying to say what ought to be achieved in twenty-first-century design. Rather, I am

describing the expanding horizons of graphic design and celebrating the breadth of contemporary practice. The immediate criticism of books such as this is that they become crib sheets for less imaginative designers; it may be the case, but I hope that if designers do lift anything from these pages, it will be the spirit and not the letter.

'experimental graphic design' has an old-fashioned ring to it, raising the spectre of early-twentieth-century modernist graphic design. In spite of these associations, however, it is still a viable term when applied to the work featured over the following pages. You are seeing here graphic research and development; arresting graphic ideas that over time will certainly cause some kind of shift in general graphic sensibility. Experimental graphic design has a momentum of its own. The designers presented here take responsibility for their work, thereby qualifying for the title of graphic author. This is a term that has been knocking around the design world for a few years now, where it is often assumed that such graphic authorship is simply about self-expression. This is not the case. If graphic designers are going to claim authorship of their output, displaying promote social wellbeing.

Cross-Disciplinary Themes
These issues are hot in the contemporary graphic-design community, but they are not solely the business of graphic designers. Responsibility and self-determination cuts across conventional disciplinary boundaries, as do other themes raised in the book. The systems explored by graphic designers are of interest to practitioners across the creative industries and beyond. The book is grouped into three categories: 'Code', 'Generic' and 'Disjunction'. Each heading is a loose description of a mode of graphic practice, and

Code

Code

One of the most significant factors promoting multi-disciplinary themes in art and design practice is the influence of new technologies. By translating information to digits, the exploration of literal and metaphorical equivalents is encouraged. Architect Daniel Libeskind, for example, employs the computer as a go-between to distill musical

rework information, other designers have examined non-digital codes, for example, Sara Maconkey borrows from DNA code to create typographic interpretations. With her DNA typeface, Maconkey accentuates the hidden relationships between our systems of information. Code has emerged as a theme of contemporary design.

Some designers keep code

neatly in its black box, so that all that is visible to us is the product of its calculations. To make images that punctuate this book, photographer Sølve Sundsbø fed information into a computer and arrived at a set of pictures suggestive of a geometrical evolution. That computer software has played a part in making these images is evident, however, all that

the intelligent manipulation of materials.

Interactivity is a key issue in almost all discussions about emergent culture. In spite of the buzz around the term, its meaning remains unfixed – it is far from conclusive how much audience participation is required before the description 'interactive' is warranted. Equally, while many of us are

in hot pursuit of the ideal of interaction, few of us are sure of its value beyond a fuzzy notion that it is a more democratic model. This is true across the board, from the most experimental art projects to culture's commercial mainstream. The significant properties of interactive TV remain a mystery even to those working within earshot of its beating heart. The projects presented here that deal most directly with the issues of interactivity are by the aptly named Tomato Interactive. Creating simple systems that offer audiences the tools to generate their own complex environments, Tomato Interactive offers a playful 'if/then' breed of interactivity that is a valuable

alternative to the stunted 'vote now/buy now' model that dominates the commercial mainstream.

is seen is but one outcome of that code. Conversely, other designers have wrenched open the black box and laid out its contents for all to see. John Maeda, professor of design and computation at MIT Media Lab, has been compared to the designers involved in the Arts and Crafts movement. His mission is to reveal the beauty of code; he

argues persuasively that, as a raw material, mathematics is invested with intrinsic qualities comparable to those of wood or clay. Maeda's elegant exploration of the computer's processes are a useful corrective. He discovers that process, even in the digital age, remains the business of

scores and mathematical formulae (among other sets of coordinates and intervals) into discrete codes, which he then weaves into his designs to invest his buildings with covert meaning. Picking up on such systems, graphic designer Paul Farrington uses software programmes to express noise – speech

and music – as animated images. The variation of regional accents becomes a formal spectrum in Farrington's work. While Libeskind and Farrington have been inspired to explore the relationships between disciplines by the fluency with which computer software can

Colorface colour font, 1999

Member of Plazm and designer of the colour font, Portland-based (Oregon, US) Joshua Berger argues that language 'is anything that communicates information'. Type is no longer merely the letters and punctuation marks that form words, sentences and paragraphs, but 'the building blocks of meaning in whatever form that meaning arises ... Type can now be an image. Type can be a sound. Type can be a color.' Adopt this view and immediately you are faced with a world that is

and unsophisticated to be considered a language. Although his argument was pedantic in many ways – his trump card was to stump people by presenting them with images of clothing articles combined in unlikely ways, a device that led him to greatly underestimate the subtlety with which we do read each other's outfits – his conclusion that language is a unique means of communication is significant.

So if typography alone is typographic, where does that leave a project like Joshua Berger's colour font

Colorface and its accompanying sound font? Made by randomly selecting colours (or notes) that are matched to letters, the font lends itself to colourful (or noisy) renditions of texts. Despite being called 'fonts', it is apparent that they are not typefaces, but alphabetic codes: the typeface is not read it is decoded.

While Berger's colour font may not be strictly typographic, it does raise pertinent questions about the nature of typographic meaning.

Bill of Rights', Berger proposes the colour of the children's show 'Teletubbies'. This may have been a one-liner, but there is a point: the Teletubbies' colours disguise the absence of any actual character traits. As representatives of rights, Teletubbies warn against constitutional fundamentalism, the tendency to forget that rights must belong to people, they do not stand alone.

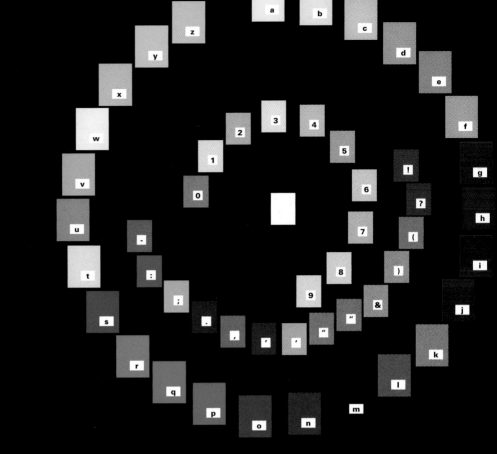

entirely typographic, everything around you becomes part of a vocabulary. Non-alphabetic typographies range from such contained, consistent systems as road markings and internationally recognized symbols, to such sprawling, unregulated sets of information as architecture and fashion.

The idea that all communication is in some sense typographic has its roots in semiology. Significantly, semiologists suggest that anything

It has long been accepted that no letterform is neutral; every typeface carries a set of meanings that has been acquired in its making and through its use. By substituting colour for form, Berger highlights the imbalances between the webs of association that attach themselves to form and colour. For the most part, while our interpretation of form is subtle and historically nuanced, our understanding of colour is an unsophisticated mish-mash of

popular psychology that calls up such clichés and childhood associations as warm oranges and cold blues.

In use, the colour font throws up other intriguing issues. Translating Guy Debord's *Society of the Spectacle*, Berger arrived at an attractive grid of colour. All surface, no depth, the grid is a metaphoric summary of the book's thesis. Less in earnest, as a short-hand colour font translation of the 'American

– symbols, images, social myths – can be read. You can extrapolate from this that if it can be read, it must be a language. One step further, it emerges that if it is a language, then its expression must be typographic.

Ultimately, whether you accept the typographic-ness of what is conventionally seen as non-typographic hinges upon whether you think that language is simply one among many other methods of communication, or whether

you believe that it holds some kind of privileged position. Furthering these ideas, anthropologist Grant McKracken tested the proposition that there might be a 'language of clothes,' by comparing how people interpret dress with how they understand speech and written language. He reasoned that our communication through clothes was far too blunt

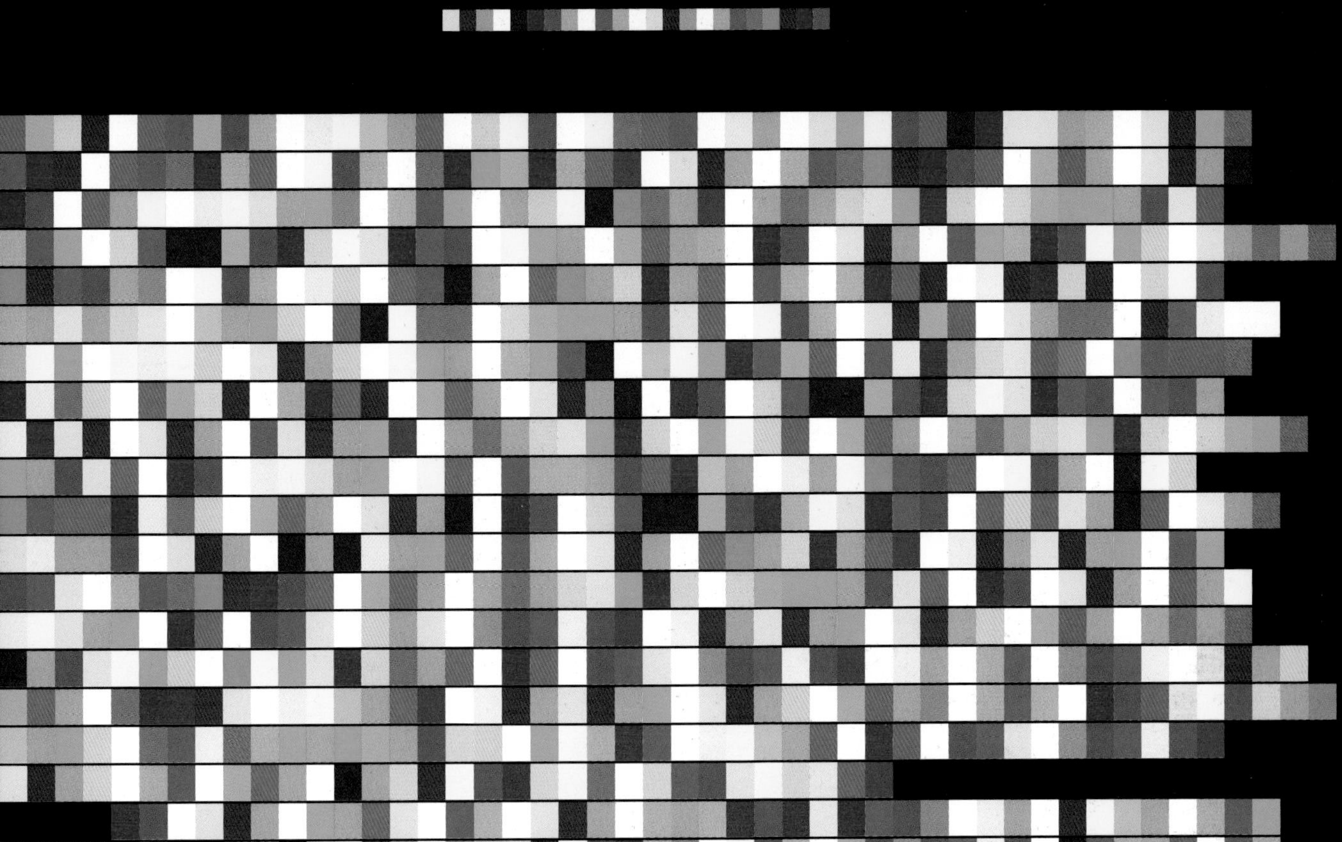

Excerpt from *Society of the Spectacle* by Guy Debord in Colorface, 1999

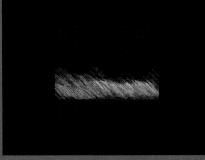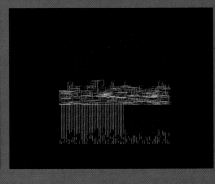

interaction of sound and image for 'Sound Polaroids'. The partners assume that the program will reveal something significant, possibly some underlying truth, about the information it has been fed. Other related assumptions are present throughout Tonne's projects. There are no absolutes in this kind of activity; the pairing of sound with image is entirely dependent on the predilections of a particular software program. So, how do you assess whether the relationship between

certain sounds and images makes sense? As Farrington points out 'it's not science'; the success of these pieces lies not in whether the marrying of sounds and images makes demonstrable sense, but rather in whether it makes experiential sense. If it works for you, then Farrington has achieved his goal.

series of imaginative sound toys that encourage playful interaction. Similarly playful are Tonne's experiments with theramins – musical instruments that generate noise in response to movement. In 1999, Farrington created 'Souton, The Yellow Voice' (overleaf), a space that contained three theramins, each connected to a computer screen. On approaching the piece, visitors realized that their movement controlled both the sound in the space and the images on the screens. In the case of relaxed participants, the outcome

was a dance between human and computer.

Farrington expanded upon these themes when he accompanied sets by experimental sound artists Scanner, Pole and SpringHeel Jack at the 'Sonic Concrete' event held at London's ICA in March 1999. Farrington moved beyond traditional club visuals – suggestive imagery, projected alongside music – to create a set of visuals that responded directly to what was being heard. Scanner and Tonne now collaborate

The main concern that runs through the work of Tonne – the experimental alter ego of London-based graphic designer Paul Farrington – is the relationship between sound and image. Traditionally, the two meet on CD production (and before that on the sleeves of vinyl records), and it was the disparity between the cover and contents of most commercial CDs that prompted Tonne to explore how sound and image could be bound together more closely. Image does more than simply illustrate

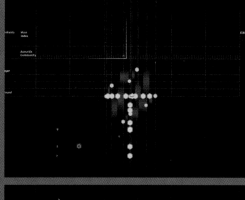
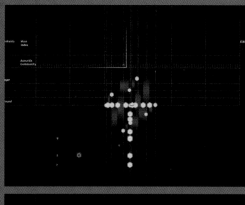
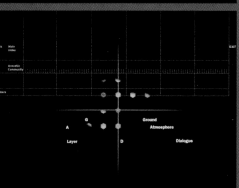
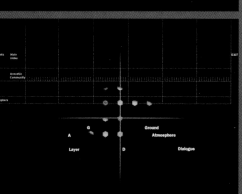
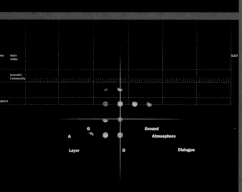
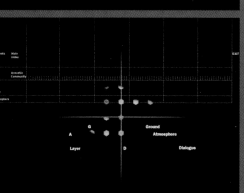
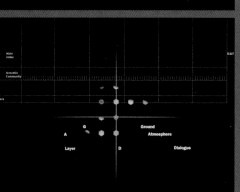

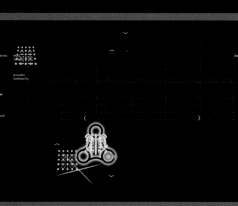
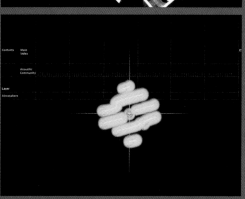

music in Farrington's work. Instead, he creates visuals that are directly generated by sound or that emit sound themselves. The pieces shown here – sound toys, installations and live music visuals – link noise and image to render them inextricable.

Tonne adopts a system that matches the audible to the visual. A grounding for much of Farrington's work, *Designs for a Deaf Audience* (1997) is a book that provides a visual representation of

four regional uk accents: Northern Ireland, Newcastle, Liverpool and Cornwall (p. 21). Participants from each region were recorded saying the alphabet, and a computer program then created a typeface from each recording. The resulting typographic environments allowed Tonne to question the role of the traditional alphabet in communication.

In 1998, his last year as a student at the Royal College of

Art, Farrington produced a set of experimental screen systems called 'Audible Communities'. On entering an audible community, users construct an audiovisual environment in which simple graphic forms and free-floating words and phrases – elliptically descriptive of the project – are partnered with pleasing, minimal sounds. Farrington has since developed these ideas into a

frequently, on live performances and in the creation of interactive audiovisual installations. Among the duo's (known as Scanner + Tonne) projects was the exhibit 'Sound Polaroids' (pp.22, 23) at the Institute of Contemporary Arts (ICA) in October 1999. Scanner + Tonne asked members of the public to nominate important London sites and subsequently made digital sound and image recordings at the most popular locations. Returning to the studio, the recordings were

processed to make them 'mutually responsive', i.e., images would automatically generate certain sounds and sound would prompt the appearance of specific images. A complex and highly technical exercise, the purpose of which was to, as Scanner + Tonne explain, 're-assemble the fragments of a city into a language born from its wow and flutter'.

Scanner + Tonne customized software to produce the unique

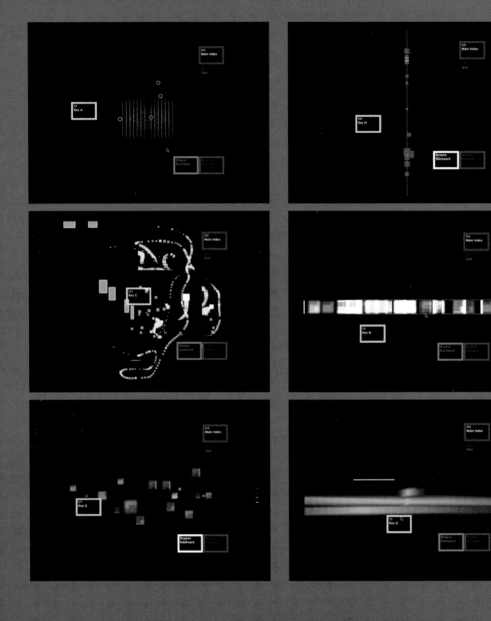

'Souton, The Yellow Voice', sound and image experiment, 1999

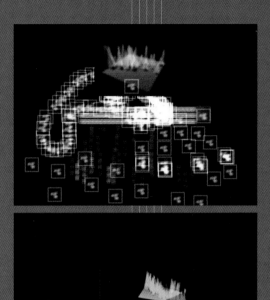

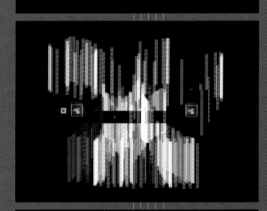

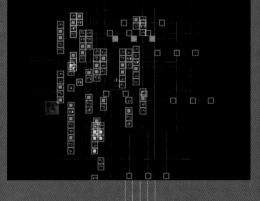

Designs for a Deaf Audience, musical representation of sound, 1997

Paul Farrington/Tonne

'Sound Polaroids' for exhibition at the ICA, London, Scanner + Tonne, 1999

DAVID CARSON
Talks about his recent work
and launches his new book
FOTOGRAFIKS.

Tuesday November 30th
Lecture Theatre 1 6:30pm

Communication Art & Design
Royal College of Art
Kensington Gore
London SW7, 2EU

David Carson is possibly the most influential graphic designer working today. He was awarded 'best use of design with photography' from the International Center for Photography, New York, and has been profiled in publications around the world, including Newsweek and the New York Times. Clients include Microsoft, Nike, MTV and Sony. Previous publications include The End of Print: The Graphic Design of David Carson and David Carson: 2nd Sight (a winner of the 77th Annual Art Directors Awards).

Carson sees photography as an extension of his activities as an internationally acclaimed graphic designer. His camera – a moderately priced point-and-shoot – is always at the ready. Experiments into spontaneity (his darkroom is the one-hour processing shop around the corner), Carson's photographs extract from the vernacular – cityscapes, graffiti, homemade graphics and signs – a rich graphic language of forms and spatial arrangements.

An essential expression of his famously original way of seeing, these photographs are curiously fleeting images seemingly lifted from their mundane context and abstracted to another realm.

Fotografiks
Text by Philip B. Meggs
Publishing and design
by David Carson

Format 232 x 288mm / 9 x 11 1/4 inch
Extent 180 pages
Text 10,000 words including captions
Illustrations 270 colour
Paper 150 gsm matt art
Binding Paperback with flaps
Price £25.00 / $34.95
Publication October 99
Laurence King Publishing
ISBN 1 85669 171 3
Gingko Press Inc 1-58423-064-5

colour with feelings is a worldwide practice; we all recognize angry red, jealous green and cool blue. Some argue that these meanings are absolute, that certain hues provoke or reflect particular moods or attitudes; others insist that they are contingent, that over time colours have come to be linked with historical and cultural expression.

However the meaning of colour has been acquired, in commercial terms it has become something to exploit. When a colour is packaged and sold, for example, as an ingredient of fashion or interior design, its associations are harnessed and revamped for promotional purposes. In the case of paint retail, new shades are given ever-more fanciful names to encourage consumers to invest hope in emulsion – to believe their freshly painted lives will be vastly more rewarding than their current shabby, peeling existence. Angry red, jealous green and cool blue are reworked as 'Passion', 'Envy' and 'Solitude'.

David Carson's book Fotografiks is a strenuously casual collection of images of the American vernacular. Taken with a point-and-shoot camera and developed at his local processing shop, the photographs display a studied spontaneity. In stark contrast, Henrik Kubel and Scott Williams's poster for a lecture to mark the book's launch is a very cool affair; 270 colour squares arranged in an incomplete 24×12 grid, headed by a text set in Helvetica that gives a technical

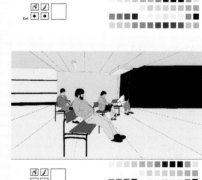

To make the 'Interactive Colouring Book', Scott Williams picked a set of paint shades with the most fantastic names (including the above three). The colouring book presents users with outlines of scenes – mostly snapshots of idealized family life, with one view of a doleful office thrown in – which they colour in using the 'utopian colour palette'. It may appear to be a closed system of bland, pre-packaged loveliness, but, in action, it offers an almost irresistible

invitation to scrawl and defile.

description of the book's content and format.

To condense the book in this decidedly non-Carsonesque manner, Kubel and Williams adopted a system in their London studio. Step one, scan the book's photographs; step two, select the first pixel (top-left-hand corner) from each scan and crop it to form a colour swatch, thus creating a single-pixel summary of all 270 images; step three, order the coloured squares according to

the sequence of the photographs in the book. Kubel and Williams have described their approach as 'surgical/minimal', an appropriate term that implies not only abstraction and restraint, but also a shearing of Carson's protrusions.

Carson's elaborate graphic style has often been criticized for promoting form at the expense of content. With this in mind, a secondary effect of replacing Carson's loud,

figurative surfaces with this kind of composition demonstrates that both are equally seductive – neither can claim a monopoly of content over form, or vice versa. That said, by failing to turn up to the lecture, Carson did not further his bid for substance above style.

Kubel and Williams have also worked on a project called the 'Interactive Colouring Book'. The association of

Speech-recognizing letterforms, 1999

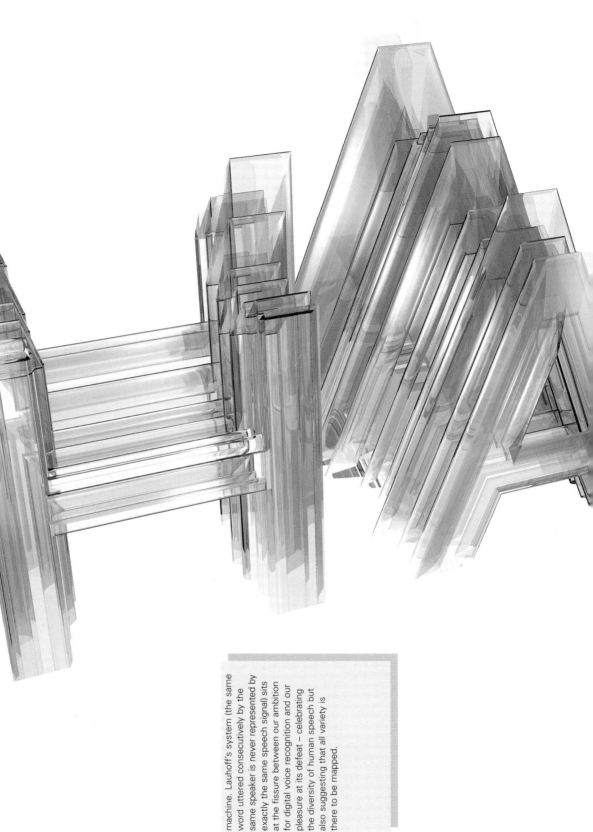

machine. Lauhoff's system (the same word uttered consecutively by the same speaker is never represented by exactly the same speech signal) sits at the fissure between our ambition for digital voice recognition and our pleasure at its defeat – celebrating the diversity of human speech but also suggesting that all variety is there to be mapped.

Compared with the spoken word, typography can often seem inexpressive. Sometimes, particularly in children's books, typographers make an effort to represent the tone of voice – big type for a shout, small type for a whisper – but there isn't a great deal of variety.

Andreas Lauhoff has taken type's muteness and has attempted to give it a human voice, using a system whereby patterns of speech can be conveyed by letterforms. He made a speech-waveform image of recorded

spoken words, dividing the
waveform into small sections that
corresponded to the enunciation
of each letter. These sections were
then rotated 45 degrees, left to
right becoming front to back, and
on the basis of their outlines three-
dimensional letterforms were
assembled.

The letterforms, made from a
transparent material that renders
their structure ever-apparent, ooze
elegant, pseudo-scientific restraint.
Not at all expressive individually,

they become so only in
comparison with each other.
Lauhoff has demonstrated the
system's potential by transcribing
a section of Stanley Kubrick's
*1968 film 2001 – A Space
Odyssey. Addressing the*
computer HAL several times,
David Bowman's tone becomes
increasingly demanding and,
as a result, Lauhoff's extruded
letterforms become larger and
more jagged.

Lauhoff's choice of human/

**computer interaction in this
instance is pertinent. His
letterforms reflect the sort
of speech that up until now
has rendered man/machine
communication fairly clumsy
outside the world of sci-fi.
However tech-friendly we
might be, there remains
something comforting about
the computer's uncertain
understanding of the spoken
word – an emblem of
humanity's resistance to the**

David Bowman saying 'HAL' the first time

Waveforms of Bowman saying 'HAL' the second time

Waveforms of Bowman saying 'HAL' the third time

*Waveforms of Bowman saying
'HAL' the fourth time*

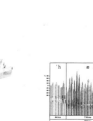

**Waveforms of Bowman saying
'HAL' the fifth time**

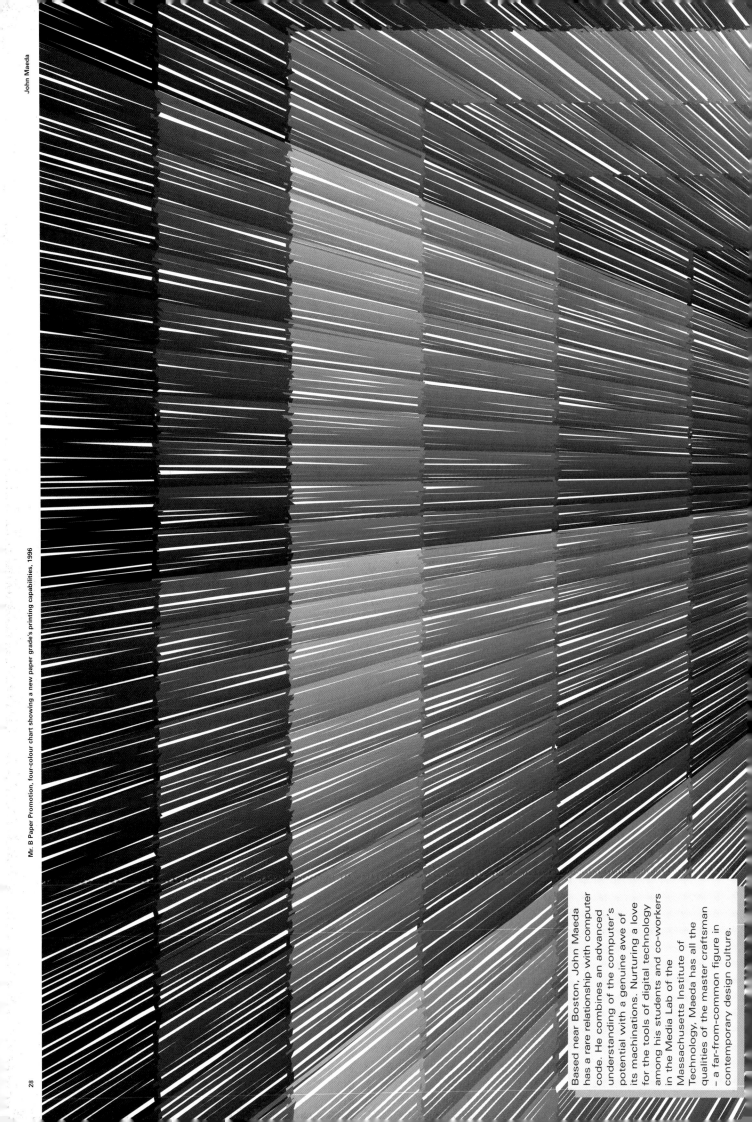

John Maeda

Mr. B Paper Promotion, four-colour chart showing a new paper grade's printing capabilities, 1996

Based near Boston, John Maeda has a rare relationship with computer code. He combines an advanced understanding of the computer's potential with a genuine awe of its machinations. Nurturing a love for the tools of digital technology among his students and co-workers in the Media Lab of the Massachusetts Institute of Technology, Maeda has all the qualities of the master craftsman – a far-from-common figure in contemporary design culture.

It is widely accepted that Maeda avoids the expressive properties of a personal graphic style and allows form to be determined by data: form follows formulae. This is not entirely true. However code-led Maeda's designs (or any graphic design, for that matter), there is obviously room for stylistic choice. Maeda's formal influences are those of late-modern American graphics – it is well known that Paul Rand (1914–96) was a significant mentor – and Japanese

poster art. To the extent that Maeda has a graphic style, it is bold, cute and exudes a direct human warmth. It is fabulous to see this range of graphic references emerging in the unexpected context of computer-driven design.

The designs shown here were devised as promotional pieces for commercial clients: Morisawa (a Japanese type foundry), Shiseido (a cosmetic company) and Sony. They demonstrate

the playful and populist nature of Maeda's thinking. That Maeda buries himself deep in the computer's 'mind' and yet emerges with designs of such universal appeal is something of a miracle; where often computer code is represented as alien and unfriendly, Maeda reveals its potential for emotion and intimacy.

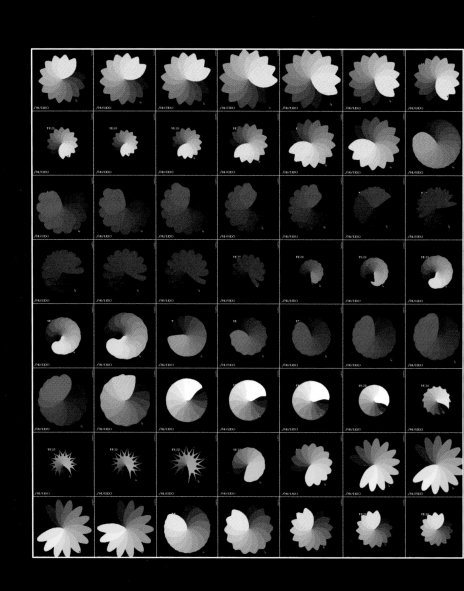

John Maeda

a 5 (poster), one of ten variants on the logotype of Japanese type foundry Morisawa, 1996

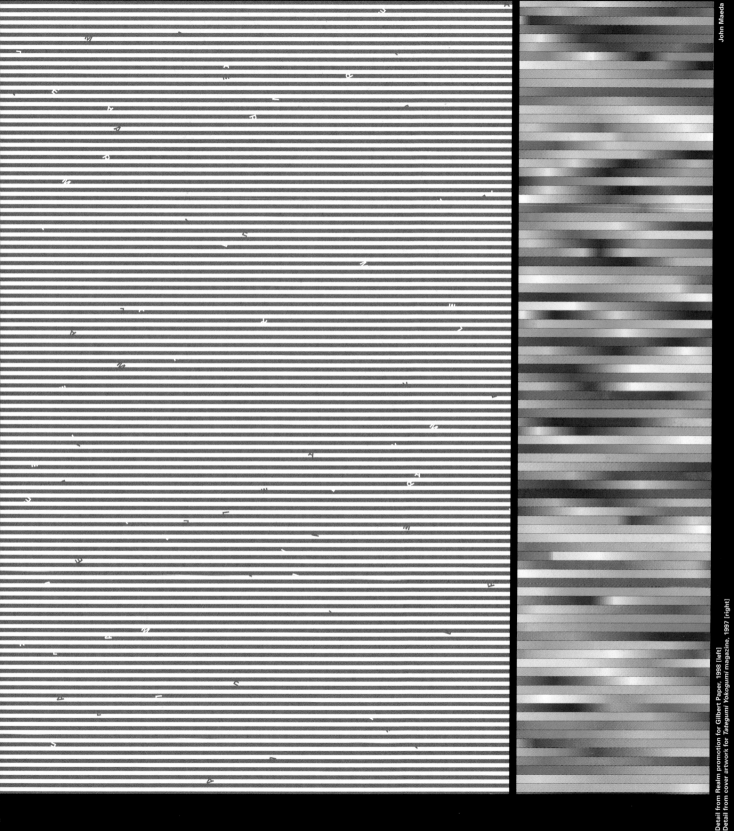

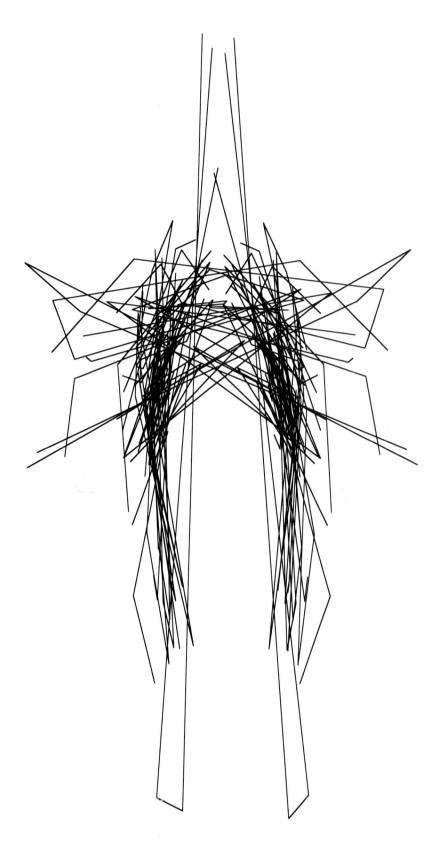

Exist typeface, 1999

Few of us can draw useful
information from alphabetic DNA
codes, yet a great many of us
are willing to believe that these
mysterious strings of letters best
portray who we are. Opaque to the
layman, DNA codes might be some
sort of incantation – maybe that is
why we are prepared to equate
our identities with these letters?

The thinking behind Sara
Maconkey's typeface Exist takes as
its starting point the idea that our
identities are described by our DNA

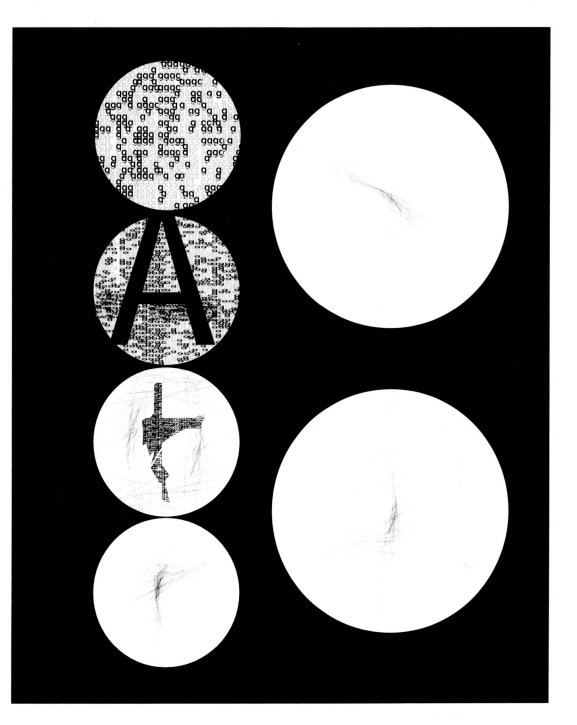

ABCDEFGHIJKLMNOP

codes. Using a DNA sequence drawn from her own insulin, Maconkey derived a typographic template that allowed her to form letters for her DNA alphabet. Maconkey claims that this complex pattern, created by joining together recurring letters of her DNA code, is the blueprint of her existence. Maconkey has suggested that the project could be developed commercially to provide personalised digital fonts'. In this way, Exist ties in neatly with the

belief that new communication technologies will promote super-customization in a future where each of us will be able to transmit and receive information that is perfectly tailored to our needs. The psychologist Sherry Turkle, author of *Life on Screen*', has argued that the stability of our identities is challenged by the proliferation of virtual worlds. Exist counteracts this instability by establishing links between our singular material existence

and our on-screen selves.
In use, Exist would enable an individual to embed complicated genetic information in the most cursory of typographic messages. Put simply, this raises the age-old concern of how who we are bears on what we say.

1. Turkle, Sherry. *Life on Screen* (New York: Simon & Schuster, 1996).

Detail from *Introduction booklet, 1999*

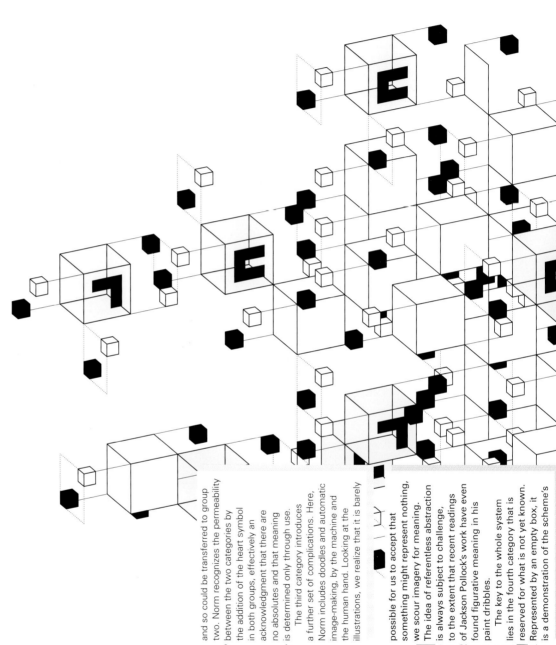

and so could be transferred to group two. Norm recognizes the permeability between the two categories by the addition of the heart symbol in both groups, effectively an acknowledgment that there are no absolutes and that meaning is determined only through use.

The third category introduces a further set of complications. Here, Norm includes doodles and automatic image-making, by the machine and the human hand. Looking at the illustrations, we realize that it is barely

possible for us to accept that something might represent nothing, we scour imagery for meaning. The idea of referentless abstraction is always subject to challenge, to the extent that recent readings of Jackson Pollock's work have even found figurative meaning in his paint dribbles.

The key to the whole system lies in the fourth category that is reserved for what is not yet known. Represented by an empty box, it is a demonstration of the scheme's

Introduction, a booklet created by Norm (Dimitri Bruni and Manuel Krebs, Zürich) to explore the aims and means of the group, presents the viewer with a paradox. The studio's method is extremely reductive – to sort and define the vocabulary of visual communication – but the outcome is highly elaborate. Putting aside the series of fluid and messy definitions that we use everyday, Norm strips away the means through which we understand the world around us to create a set of perfect and neatly bound categories. Unsurprisingly, the world does not fit into these categories without putting up a fight, and the result of this struggle, evident on the pages of *Introduction*, is a complex profusion of simplicity.

Norm has formed four categories of graphic representation: 1) things that represent something in three-dimensional space; 2) things that represent something two-dimensional; 3) things that

flaws. What at first glance may have seemed to be a project directly related to the pursuit of absolute graphic meaning, a project associated with the modernist designers of the Swiss school, begins to appear as something quite different. Apparently engaged in the activity of defining and containing, the designers allow their own program to unravel in category four.

represent something that is neither three-dimensional nor two-dimensional, but refers only to itself; 4) the group of things that are not yet known, a group reserved for the exceptional or unexpected.

At first these definitions seem clear, but as soon as they are put into use problems occur. For example, abstract logotypes – of the kind so beloved by corporate modernists – are slotted into category two. Norm has created

a few of these logotypes from scratch to use as examples, but even these, designed to be case studies in abstraction, possess a figurative element that might merit their placement in group one. Equally, it could be argued that some of the symbols in group one, diagrammatic reductions of three-dimensional objects, have an entirely independent two-dimensional existence

MNOPQR

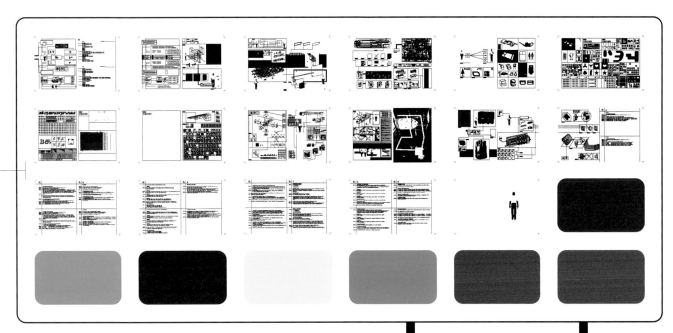

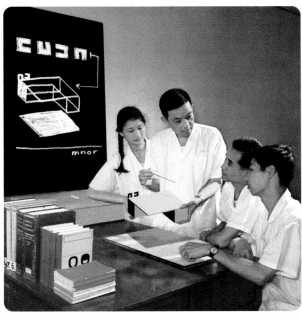

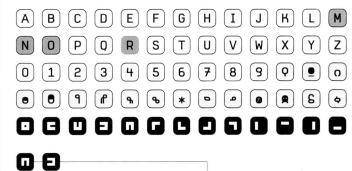

POSITION.1

POSITION.2

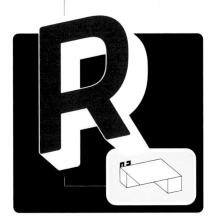

NORM:INTRODUCTION >BOOK

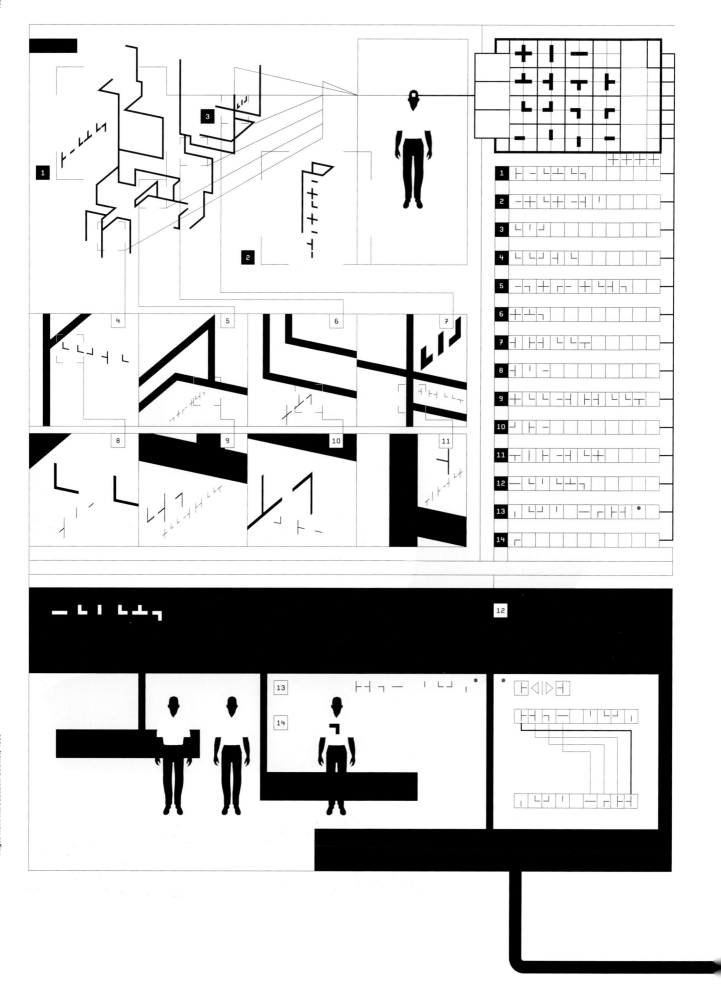

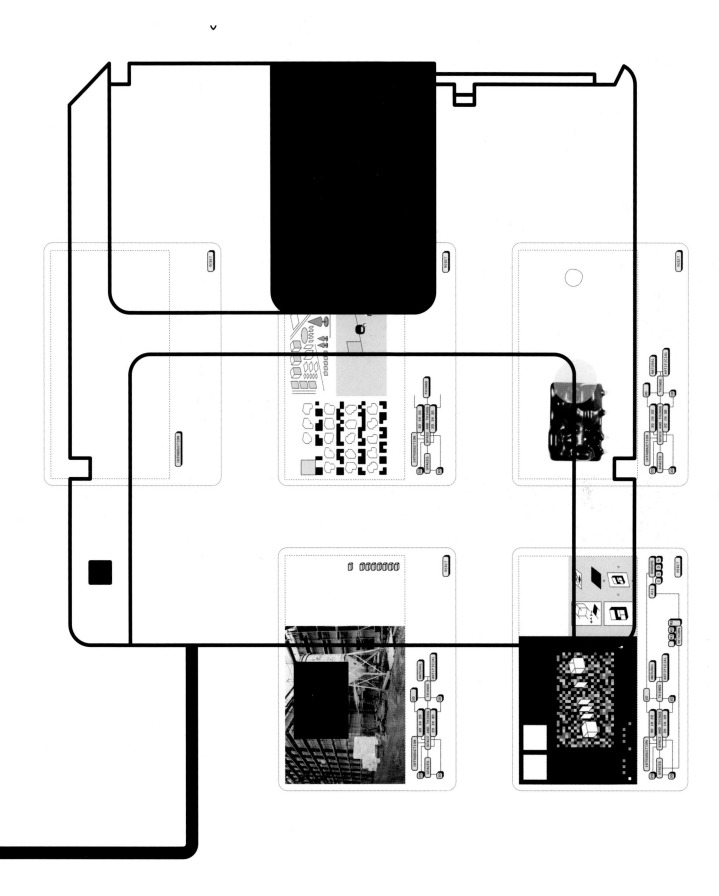

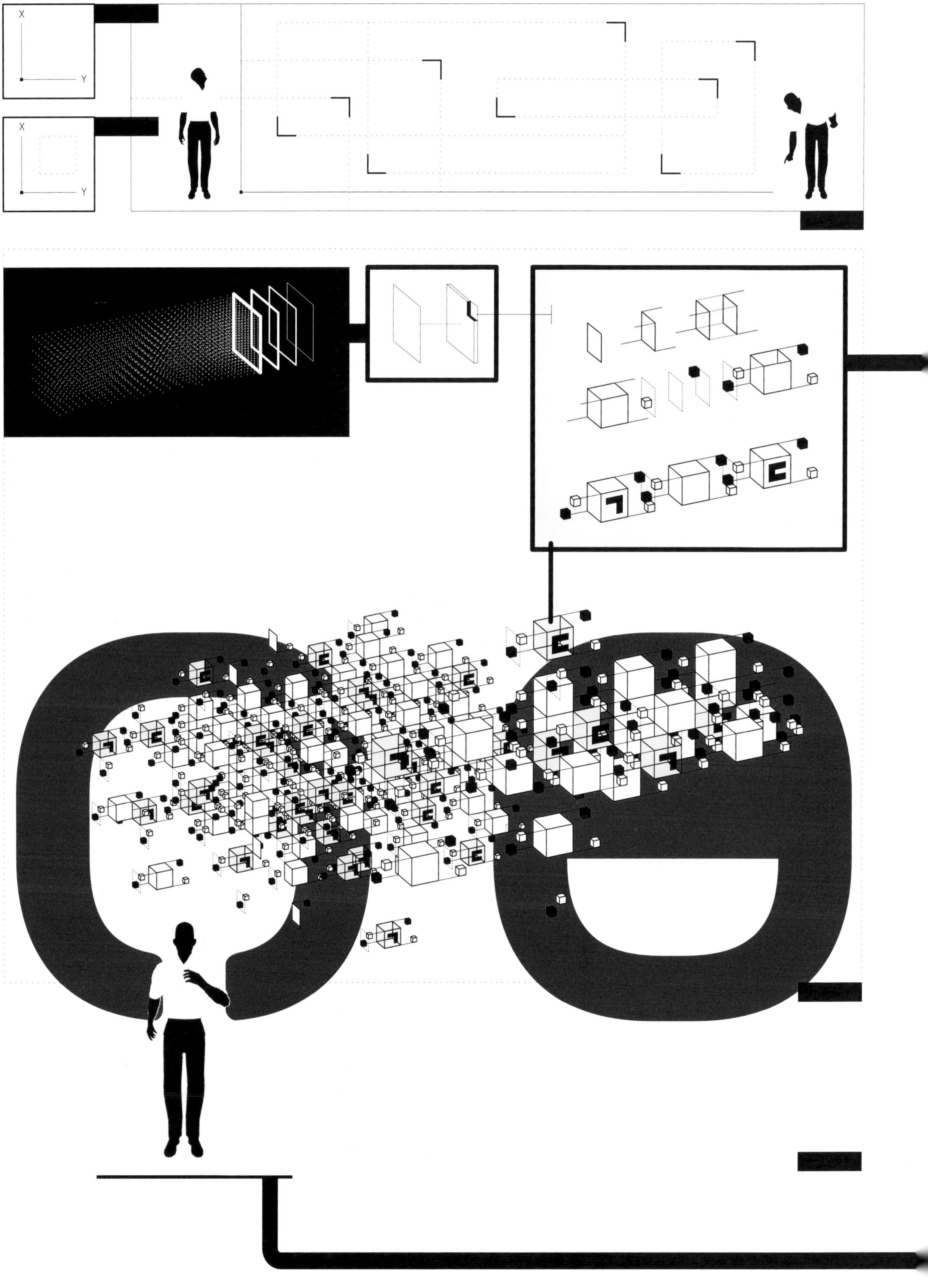

Pages from *Introduction* booklet, 1999

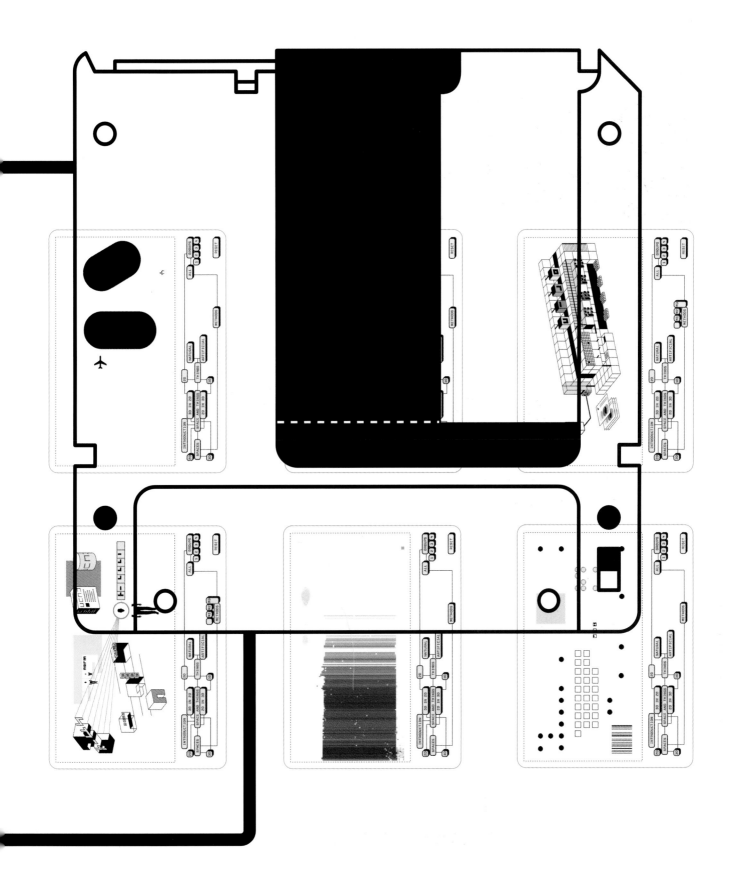

inside
> inside ^floors^
> > inside ^wire^
> > > inside ^fill^

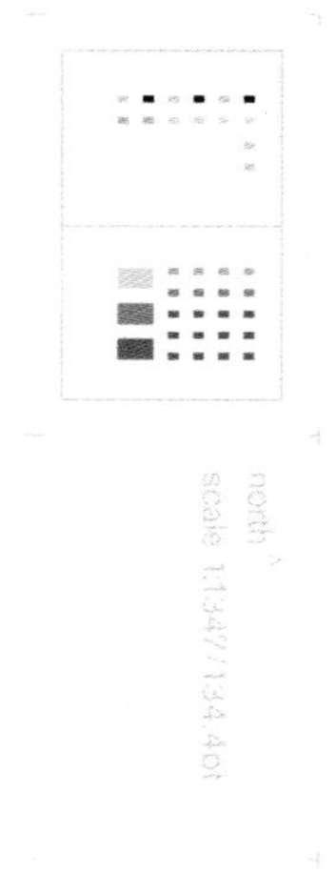

north ^
scale 1:1347/134.4pt

space
> space ^mass^
> space ^fill^
> > space ^wire^

plan
> plan ^floors^
> plan ^wire^
> > plan ^fill^

north ^

north ^

One of the most fundamental questions raised by Steinbrüchel's work is whether the translation of architectural structure into typographic form really is the best expression of the spirit of Libeskind's building. Experimentation in different fields of design has run in parallel for many years; Steinbrüchel implies that these fields must become more integrated before their revolutionary potential can be realized.

The most important lettering, the new lettering we need to create, is that which is conceived as part of the architecture to which it belongs, which from the expressionist point of view therefore epitomises the idea of the building.
NICOLETE GRAY
(*Lettering on Buildings*, 1960)

What relationship should lettering have with the architectural environment? Using Daniel Libeskind's planned extension to London's Victoria and Albert Museum as a case study. Ralph Steinbrüchel (based in Zürich) has taken up Nicolete Gray's long-standing challenge and has proposed a new partnership between architecture and typography.

Libeskind's design is a radical venture – The Spiral dismantles conventional architectural structures and recombines them in a startling fashion. To achieve unity of expression between architecture and typography, Steinbrüchel has used Libeskind's plans as a lens through which to filter letterforms. The outcome is an alphabet strung together from a series of jarring and discontinuous shapes. Using this typeface inside The Spiral would result in stylistic harmony, and signs would carry far more information than their immediate message.

In answer to critics who might argue that architectural typography is unreadable, Steinbrüchel insists that it is consistency of application rather than conventionality of form that renders type legible. Drawing on an architectural metaphor, he suggests that just as the spaces of a building only make sense in the context of the structures around them, so letters only make sense as part of an applied typography.

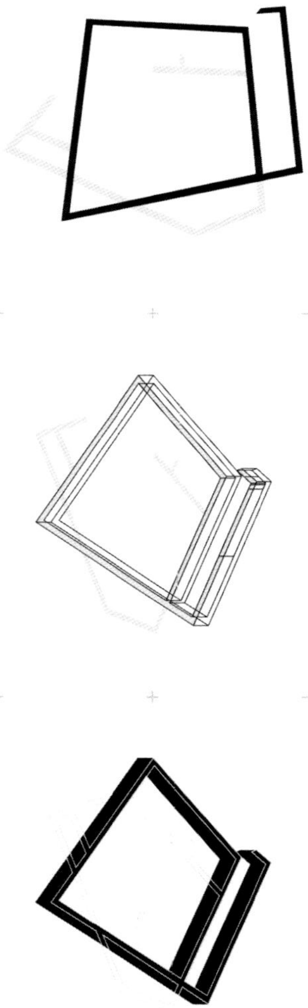

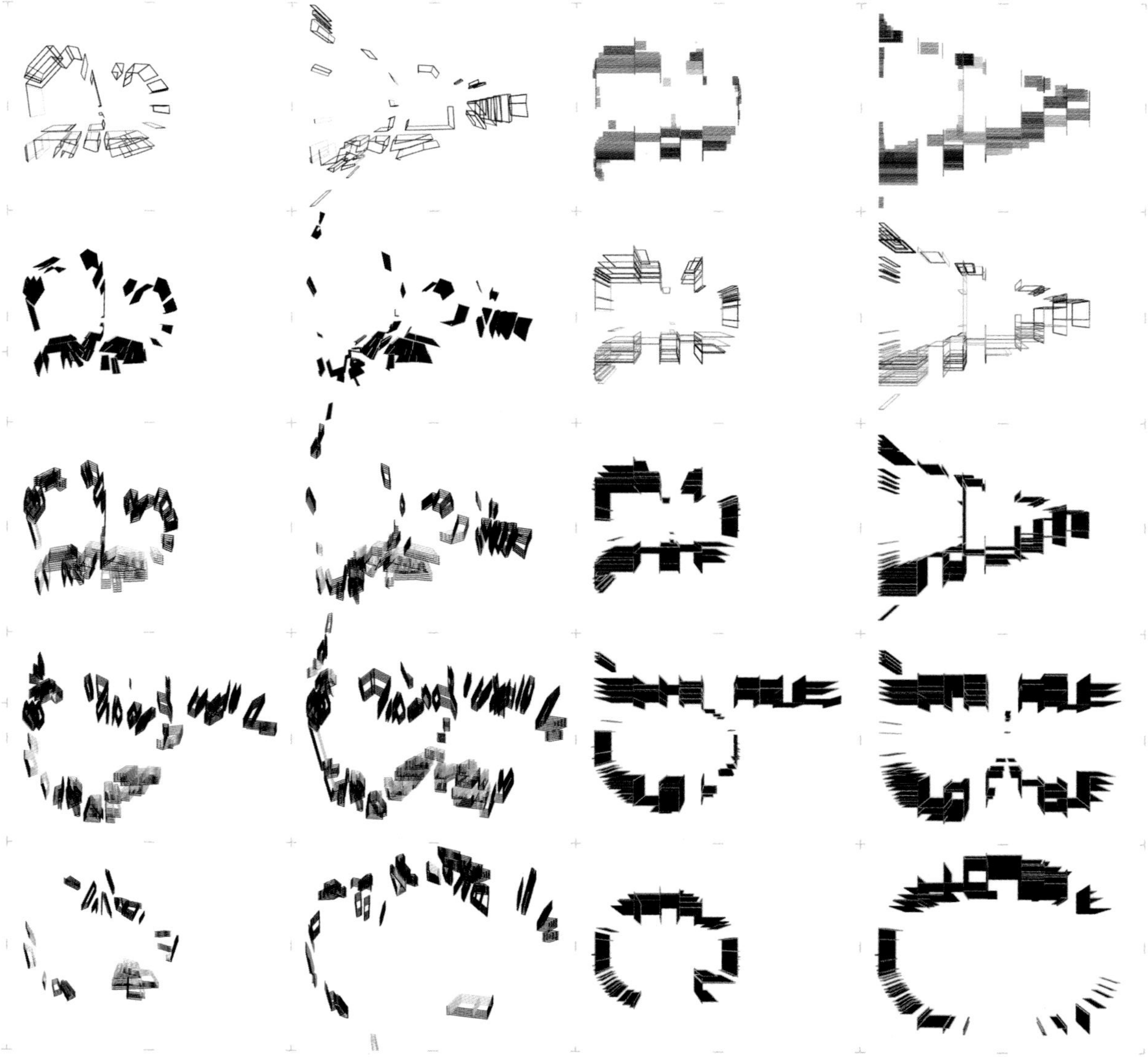

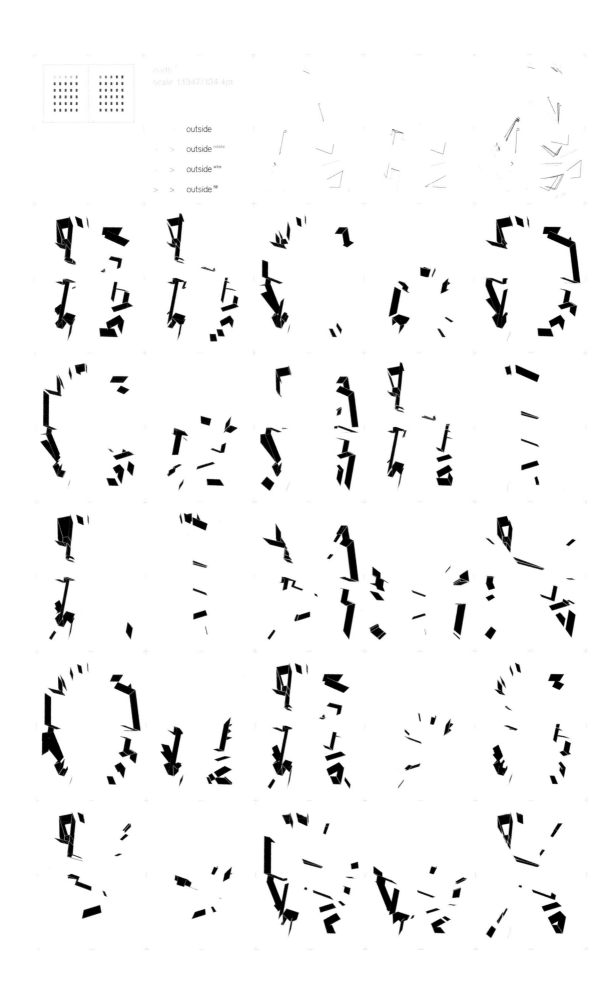

outside

> outside rotate

> outside wire

> > outside fill

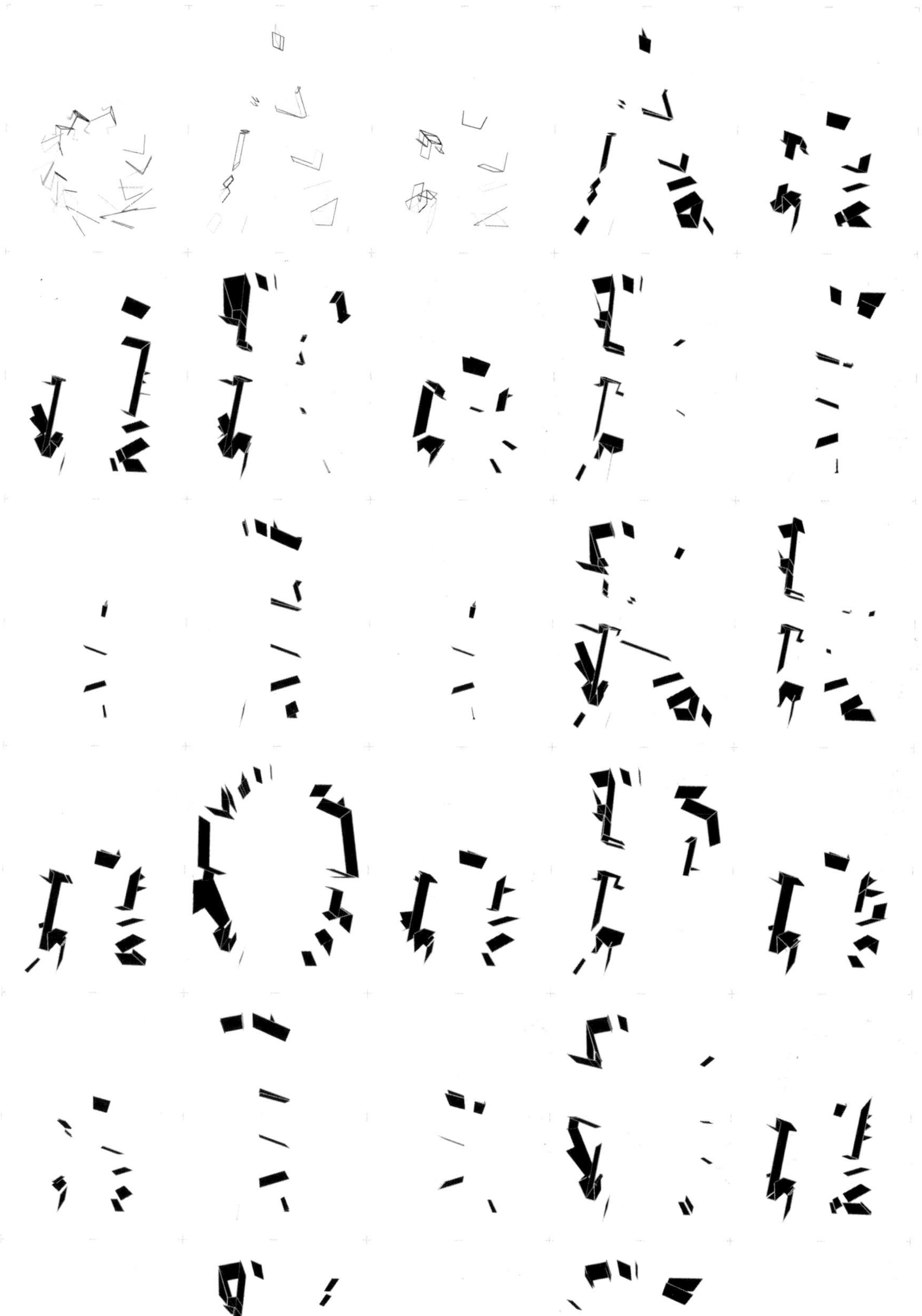

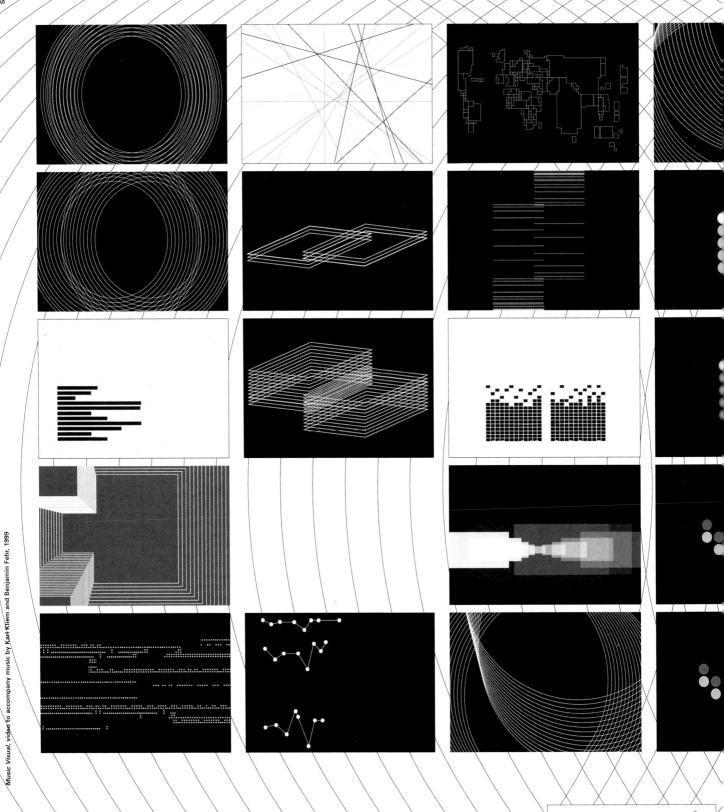

Music Visual, video to accompany music by Karl-Kliem and Benjamin Fehr, 1999

Developed in tandem, Stefanie Barth's visual and Karl Kliem and Benjamin Fehr's music mimic one another in approach. Both are built, piece by piece, from a narrow repertoire of elements and both eschew the high tech and complex in favour of the low tech and minimal. Barth (Frankfurt) has created a video that pulses in time with the music. It shows a series of simple, animated geometric devices that appear at intervals determined by the structure of the musical composition.

The twinning of geometric pattern and minimal electronic music may seem very appropriate to a contemporary audience, but the relationship between the two cannot be assumed. The title of Barth's piece *Music Visual* refers to the animated films of Oskar Fischinger (1900–67), a pioneer of experimental cinema. Fischinger's animations of the 1920s and 1930s were pared down and abstract (as are Barth's), but his forms danced in time to such pre-existing orchestral compositions as Johannes Brahms's *Hungarian Dances* – very unlike the minimal music of Kliem and Fehr.

The visual and auditory aesthetic of *Music Visual* is a counterpoint to the sensory overload delivered by most mainstream music and music videos. It may be that the successful partnership of sound and image as shown here is a result of a joint reaction against dominant contemporary modes.

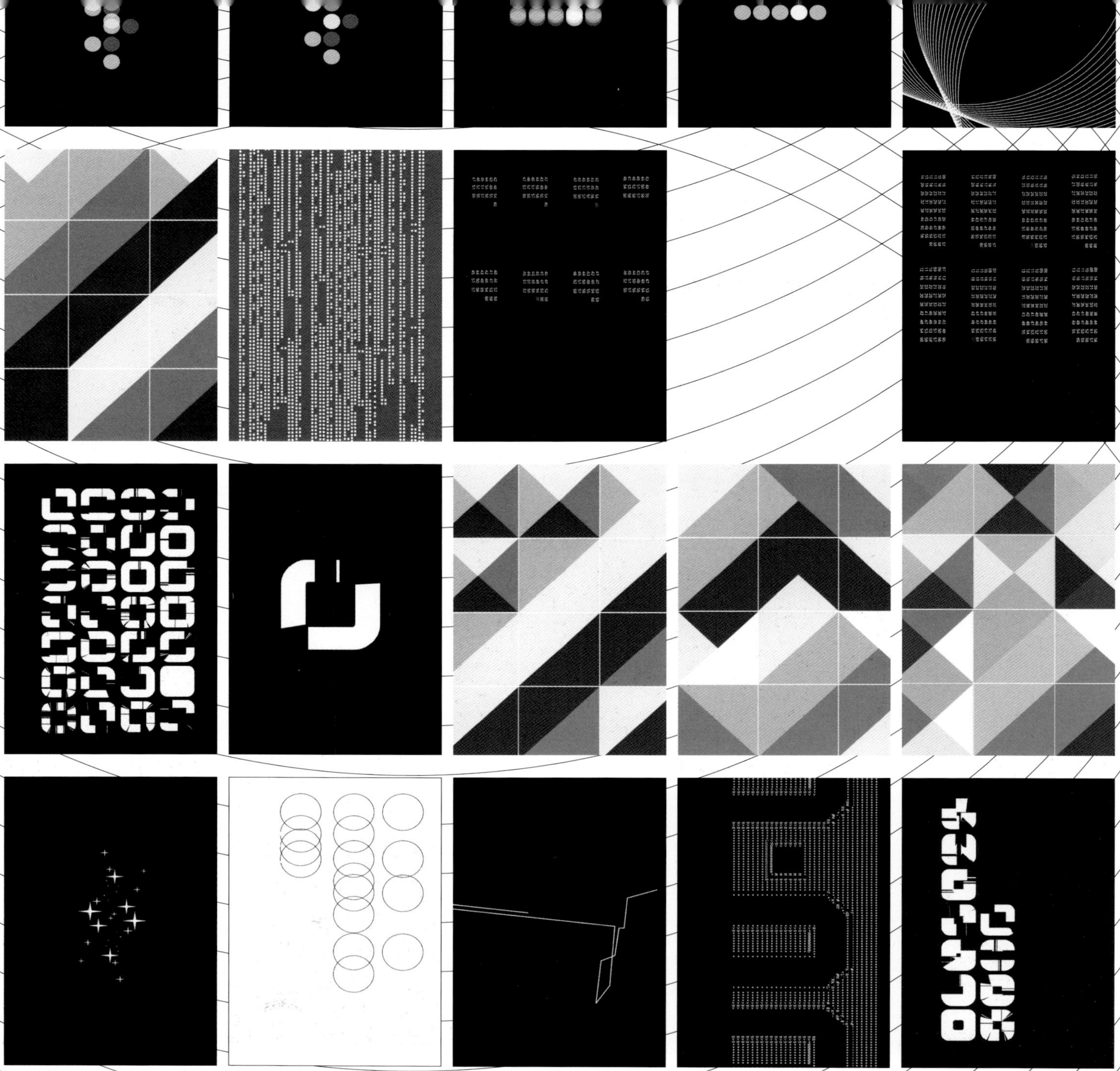

'Jam' exhibition, Anti-rom, London, 1996

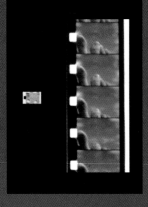

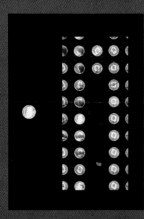

simple generative systems in which users build up complex, customized environments from minimal materials – fragments of sound, image or pattern. While mainstream interactive models appear to have petrified into the click-here/vote-now/buy-now model, Tomato Interactive's work remains fluid and expansive.

In spite of the inordinate amount of time that huge numbers of people spend in front of computer screens, good screen practice – the most successful composition and navigation of on-screen media – remains an uncertain business. Possibly the best piece of advice to emerge from all the years spent gazing at blinking dots of light is that there can be no single model. Pioneers of interactive design (in the late-1980s, early-1990s) were very keen to overturn the

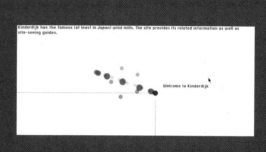

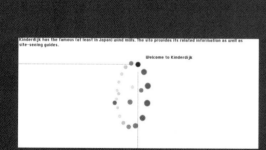

preconception of the screen as page; simply clicking your way through a succession of singular screen images was regarded as a criminal waste of interactive potential. This led to a host of experiments into fuzzy interactivity – on-screen environments that encouraged users to wander at random through what were most often fields of bouncing and bleeping form (a blurry-edged aesthetic became almost obligatory).

These environments are still around (and are still pleasant to spend time in), but they have been joined by a number of sharper-edged models. The London design group Tomato Interactive (comprising three former members of Anti-rom, a design team who were virtuosos of the bounce and bleep) explore how navigation systems allow multiple routes, but nonetheless permit users to arrive purposefully at a single point.

In the system the group has developed for Sony Vaio Net, each one of a set points arranged in a rotating circle takes the user to a different outer circle, which likewise consists of a number of dots. Significantly, once inside the system, the user is only two clicks away from any one of over a hundred links.
In their more playful work, the members of Tomato Interactive experiment with

Generic

Generic

A great many contemporary graphic designers are concerned with the generic, the ordinary, the everyday. Not content to let familiar graphic languages rest, studios such as Anthony Burrill and Graphic Thought Facility (GTF) subject them to systematic distortion and amplification with offbeat and arresting results. GTF's aim to 'extract the juice' from

insistence that everyday forms carry meaning too! Now such arguments seem somewhat tired, old hierarchies of form have been challenged and designers and artists can explore the entire formal range without being obliged to praise or to deride it.

The issue of utility cuts across artistic disciplines and sits alongside the refreshed

envelope; and a furniture collection in which loose covers become dresses, chairs fold into suitcases and a table telescopes into a circular skirt. Artist Andrea Zittel has also investigated the idea of utility. She has invented a basic garment called a personal panel, and has illustrated herself engaged in a number of everday tasks wearing different panels made

from fabrics of various colours and patterns. Zittel's drawings have a persuasive, reductive charm and, like the designs of Miyake and Chalayan, ask teasing questions about what might make our lives complete, what might be the last item we would ever have to buy.

The typographic identity system designed for the

WALKER DESIGNED FOR
THE WALKER ARTS CENTER

all basic typographic needs, but in use the typeface looks quirky and eccentric. A further example of graphic utility comes from Swiss design group Müller + Hess – a Swiss contribution to this discussion is particularly appropriate as the idea of a singular, economic graphic solution to all graphic problems is most strongly associated with the

and Hess promote a brand of ad-hoc functionality that has obvious contemporary relevance.

the everyday has strong parallels with designers outside the graphics field, for example, Jasper Morrison has won acclaim for creating furniture of disarming ordinariness and exaggerated normality. Similarly, the artist Julian Opie has applied a pared-down, comic-book aesthetic to portraiture and landscape,

use of the generic. After a long period of disillusionment with the modernist ideal, designers and artists have begun to rephrase questions concerning the economy of means and basic human need. Fashion designers Issey Miyake and Hussein Chalayan have explored this theme in different ways. Miyake has created a cut-out outfit kit

design that emerged from postwar Switzerland. Müller and Hess invent ingenious systems whereby information and communicative texture emerge from repeated overprinting. They use cheap and readily available paper stocks and set up grid systems that can hold uneven bodies of text without smoothing over their irregularities. Müller

that allows the wearer to make her own clothes from a single tube of scored and seamed fabric. Chalayan, on the other hand, has produced a series of extraordinary multi-purpose items, such as the air-mail dress, a garment made from a light but hard-wearing fabric that can be packed into an

Walker Art Center by Matthew Carter in 1995 is a graphic-design parallel. Coming as a kit of parts, the basic forms of the Walker typeface can be augmented with such features as serifs and underscores, providing a pleasingly off-centre take on a singular solution. Walker economically fulfils

mining visual assumption for fresh meaning. When Opie first employed this method in the early 1990s, discussions about his work suggested that it was either a critique - an exploration of the poverty of bleak postwar modernity - or an affirmation - the

XXXEROX, Levis campaign, 1998 [top]
You Are Here [sticker], 1997 [bottom]

divorcees' crockery set. Morgan and
Watson intend to sell these products
on their website Bumptown.co.uk,
thereby offering means of communication
directly to a wordshy public.

Bump is made up of designers Jon
Morgan and Mike Watson. Their
task is basic communication, a task
that is not so different from the
most traditional of graphic-design
objectives. But where designers
have striven for decades to deliver
messages of corporate or social
benefit, Bump try to tell it how it is.
They are not informing us that IBM
is a visionary company, they are not
encouraging us to recycle paper and
they are not advising us to turn right
to reach Luton by the A505. They

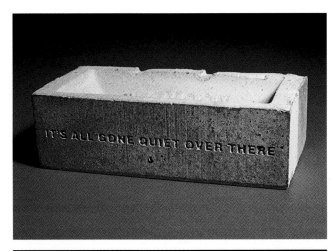

MY OTHER BAG'S A
LOUIS VUITTON

Bricks for 'Stealing Beauty' exhibition at the ICA, London, 1999 [left]
'Shopping' (carrier bag), 1999 [right]

aim to make explicit what is going on right here, right now: 'You're going home in a fucking ambulance'; 'Where's your caravan'; 'Come and have a go if you think you're hard enough'; 'It's all gone quiet over there'. The messages are shot-blasted on ordinary house bricks; form and content working in perfect harmony.

One of the fundamental aspects of London-based Bump's work is Britishness – the idea of the British

individual, buttoned up, yet bubbling over with rage and inanity. Needless to say this is a stereotype, but it is not without mileage. Most British people know what it is to seethe with suppressed anger, and the designers are not alone in their implication that violence may be the flipside of inhibition. They specialize in nasty, mean-spirited representations of the ordinary public.

Bump's bricks were made in

1999 as part of 'Stealing Beauty', an exhibition of British design at London's Institute of Contemporary Art (ica). As communication methods they do not have an immediate (or legal) application, although they have been filmed in glass-breaking action for a TV show about men's fashion. That has not, however, stopped Bump pursuing related projects, for instance, a

Ugly strikes one in three

Calling cards, line drawings, 1998 [this page and opposite]

Ahead Only, self-published book [this page and opposite], 1998

WAITING FOR REPLY

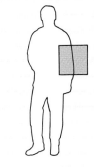

understood graphic language using abstract form. Read negatively, these images demonstrate the stubborn opacity of graphic meaning: read positively, they suggest that it is possible to adopt the generic and imbue it with personal messages.

REDUCE SPEED NOW

In print, London-based Anthony Burrill takes the ordinary and makes it loud. Turn up the visual volume, way past comfort level, and soon the generic is quite alien. In Burrill's book *Ahead Only*, clumsy bitmap typefaces – like those showing Ceefax information on TV screens – turn into aggressive, jagged landscapes and the bland messages that they spell out ('Fresh Cut Flowers in Next Lay-by') become bombastic and unreasonable commands. Pictorially, simple line

ever site, the site that stood at the dawn of the Web. To that end, Burrill and his programming partner Kip Parker have created a nest of reassuringly low-tech imagery and fuzzy digital sound. Pressing reliable nostalgia buttons (such as a reference to the 1970s computer game Pong), Friendchip encourages reverie of the past in an arena that is for the most part relentlessly new. Primitive by choice, Friendchip reaps the rewards of opting for unsophisticated form – Web toys load quickly and are

responsive and fun. Suddenly the big digit does not seem so wilful – it begins to expose the huge gap between what we expect of the Internet and what it can actually deliver. Burrill's approach raises significant questions about what might be involved in building a new medium from scratch.

The most enigmatic motifs in Burrill's work appear in his book *Men and Shapes* (overleaf). Print and screen versions show silhouette figures – sometimes entirely cloaked

Kraftwerk website (top), 1999

FRESH CUT FLOWERS IN NEXT LAY-BY

in black and at other times distinguished by basic colours – accompanied by geometric forms. Two films consider encounters between men and geometrical form. In Stanley Kubrick's 1968 *2001: A Space Odyssey*, monkeys and men are altered by their proximity to a large, rectangular, smooth-sided monolith. Two years later Woody Allen's film *Sleeper*, essentially a parody of *2001*, shows men and women of the future deriving pleasure from a sphere the size of

a beach ball and known as 'Orb'. Really deep or really silly, meetings between men and shapes are charged with meaning. The outline figures in *Men and Shapes* echo early James Bond title sequences – they are both generic action men (and women) and identifiable characters. The geometric forms superimposed upon these figures refer back to a time when it seemed possible to create a universally

drawings are recast as strange emblems: they might be establishing new codes of conduct, unfamiliar social rules, yet they withhold any workable information. Burrill's schemes all use the technique of displacement, he takes the normal and makes it strange.

On screen, Burrill's projects could be a corrective to our long-standing infatuation with technology and our ceaseless adoption of the new. He forces us to revisit our first encounters with

new media and prevents us from taking any mode of communication for granted. In the mid-1980s, a generation of graphic pioneers battled with early desktop-publishing programs, struggling to create form from unwieldy digits. These pioneers, among them Emigre founder and type designer Zuzana Licko, were later dubbed 'techno-primitives'. Making bitmap letterforms that are strongly reminiscent of Licko's

early digital alphabets, such as Oakland and Emperor, Burrill could be part of a new generation of techno-primitives. Unlike Licko, however, for whom upgrades were not an option, Burrill chooses to work with equipment that he calls 'crappy'. His primitivism is elective not compulsory.

The Friendchip website is intended to give the impression of being the first

Men and Shapes, self-published book, 1999

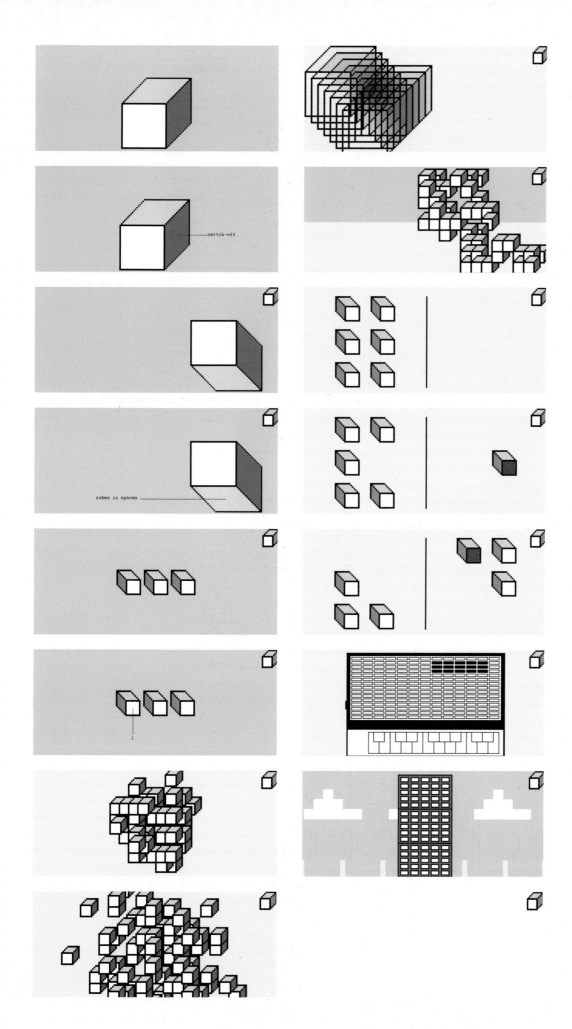

Playground, interactive website, 1999

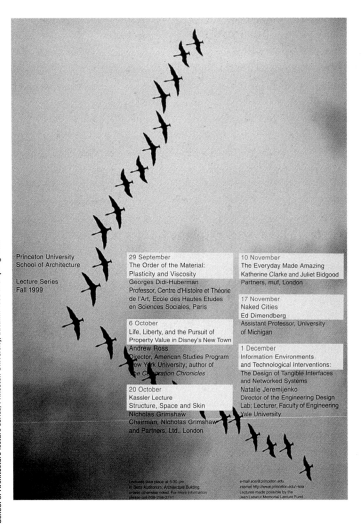

Princeton University
School of Architecture

Lecture Series
Fall 1999

29 September
The Order of the Material:
Plasticity and Viscosity
Georges Didi-Huberman
Professor, Centre d'Histoire et Théorie
de l'Art, Ecole des Hautes Etudes
en Sciences Sociales, Paris

6 October
Life, Liberty, and the Pursuit of
Property Value in Disney's New Town
Andrew Ross
Director, American Studies Program
New York University; author of
the Celebration Chronicles

20 October
Kassler Lecture
Structure, Space and Skin
Nicholas Grimshaw
Chairman, Nicholas Grimshaw
and Partners, Ltd., London

10 November
The Everyday Made Amazing
Katherine Clarke and Juliet Bidgood
Partners, muf, London

17 November
Naked Cities
Ed Dimendberg
Assistant Professor, University
of Michigan

1 December
Information Environments
and Technological Interventions:
The Design of Tangible Interfaces
and Networked Systems
Natalie Jeremijenko
Director of the Engineering Design
Lab; Lecturer, Faculty of Engineering
Yale University

Lectures take place at 5:30 pm
in Betts Auditorium, Architecture Building;
unless otherwise noted. For more information
please call 609-258-3741

e-mail soa@princeton.edu
internet http://www.princeton.edu/~soa
Lectures made possible by the
Jean Labatut Memorial Lecture Fund

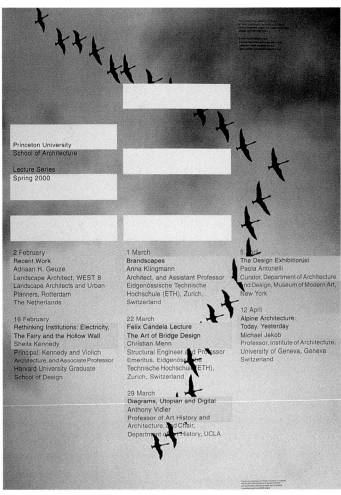

Princeton University
School of Architecture

Lecture Series
Spring 2000

2 February
Recent Work
Adriaan H. Geuze
Landscape Architect, WEST 8
Landscape Architects and Urban
Planners, Rotterdam
The Netherlands

16 February
Rethinking Institutions: Electricity,
The Fairy and the Hollow Wall
Sheila Kennedy
Principal; Kennedy and Violich
Architecture, and Associate Professor
Harvard University Graduate
School of Design

1 March
Brandscapes
Anna Klingmann
Architect, and Assistant Professor
Eidgenössische Technische
Hochschule (ETH), Zurich,
Switzerland

22 March
Felix Candela Lecture
The Art of Bridge Design
Christian Menn
Structural Engineer and Professor
Emeritus, Eidgenössische
Technische Hochschule (ETH),
Zurich, Switzerland

29 March
Diagrams, Utopian and Digital
Anthony Vidler
Professor of Art History and
Architecture, and Chair,
Department of Art History, UCLA

5 April
The Design Exhibitionist
Paola Antonelli
Curator, Department of Architecture
and Design, Museum of Modern Art,
New York

12 April
Alpine Architecture:
Today, Yesterday
Michael Jakob
Professor, Institute of Architecture,
University of Geneva, Geneva
Switzerland

In the first of his posters for Princeton School of Architecture in autumn 1999, Elliman (Connecticut, US) flowed the information about the lecture series into a set of text boxes arranged atop a photograph of migrating geese.

For the second poster, Elliman flipped the same image top to bottom and left to right. Deleting the text about the first series, he left the boxes floating over the flying geese. By inserting information about the new series in a second

conditions. These activities are mirrored in major and minor cities all over the world, from Seattle and Tokyo to Fayetteville in Arkansas.

Paul Elliman created an 'identity' for Critical Mass by borrowing the logo and slogan from American recycling bins. Reworking the phrase 'We Recycle' to 'We Cycle', Elliman offers a critique of mainstream environmental activity, summed up by him as 'two cars in the garage and a blue recycling bin out front'.

Critical Mass is not an organization in any traditional sense of the word; there is no central office and, although Internet communication is essential to activists, there is no single website. In turn, Elliman's identity is not an identity in any traditional sense of the word. Its purpose is not to communicate a singular message, rather it is a graphic expression of the group's broad rejection of corporate and government values.

To paraphrase Elliman, the A–Z map cut into arrows (overleaf)

WE CYCLE
Critical Mass

T-shirt for environmental group Critical Mass, 1999

suggests the wind direction given by weather forecasters and the reorganized/disorganized maps of Paris that were assembled in the 1950s by situationist Guy Debord. However, Elliman's maps are more intended as a tribute to Phyllis Pearson, the founder of the London A–Z street guides, who cycled across the city to verify each road, path and cul-de-sac that was included in the guide.

set of yellow text boxes, Elliman produced a relatively busy poster that not only gave details of the second lecture series but also acted as a record of the first.

The posters evoke almost contradictory themes. The first is palimpsest, the belief that the present bears the indelible imprint of the past – an idea that is effectively a cliché of postmodern thought. The second is the cycle, the conviction that the present moment is simply one point in

an endlessly repeated circle of activity. To talk about palimpsest is an assertion of the uniqueness of the historical course; to refer to the cycle amounts to an insistence on a commonality that is achieved through an irresistible, natural order. Maybe the contradiction acts as a metaphor for the academic institution, a place where individuals tread unique paths through seasonally repeated courses.

Critical Mass is an informal gathering of groups and individuals who share a range of environmental concerns. On the last Friday evening of every month Critical Massers travel through London, mostly by bicycle, to occupy such areas as Trafalgar Square, Parliament Square, Park Lane and Piccadilly Circus in a bid to raise awareness of the city's appalling road and air

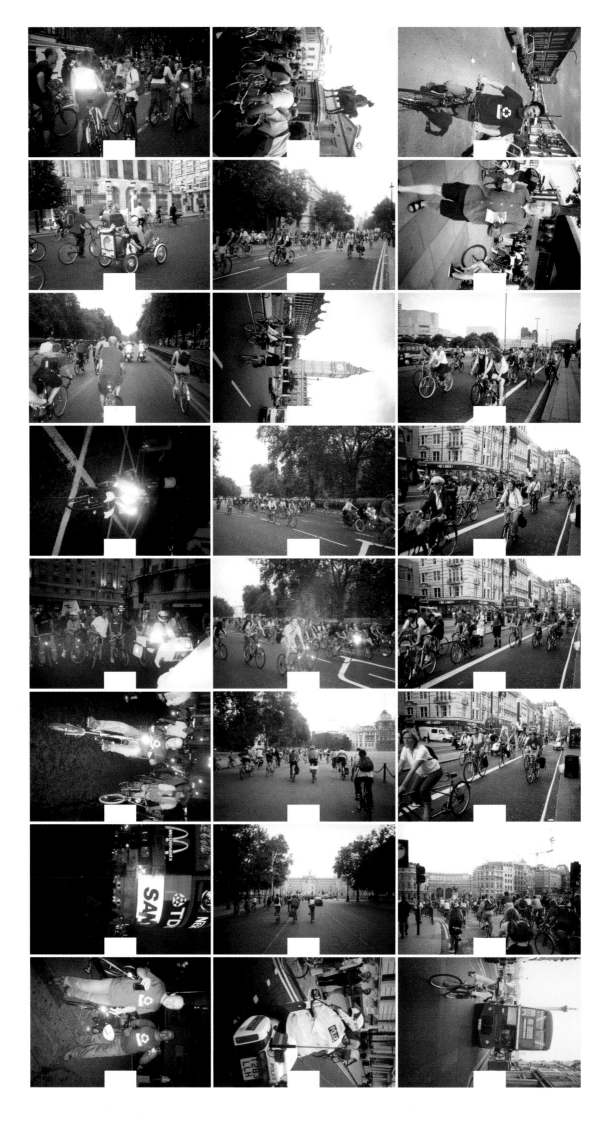

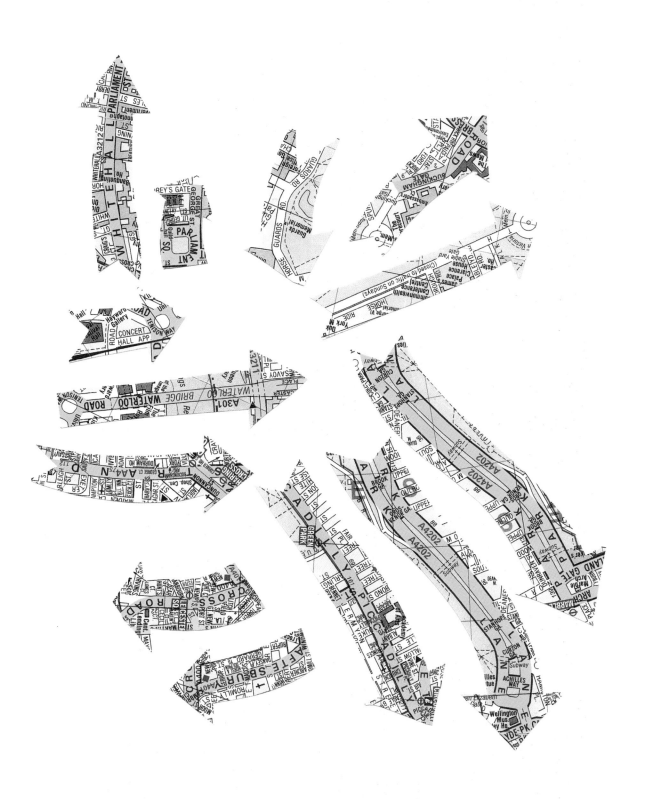

A–Z map cut into directional arrows, 2000

GO-SEES book, 1999

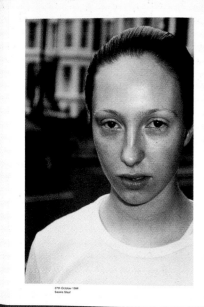

27th October 1998
Saskia Staf

27th October 1999
Karen Quinn

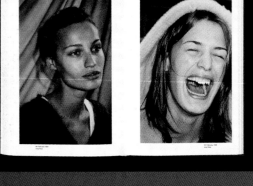

increasingly important corporate and retail presence on the Web. Apart from being an idealized, democratic space, Wow Wow is also visually interesting. MMS (Fuel) use downloaded imagery to good effect and by so doing obscure the visually turgid truth of online experience. Wow Wow contains the occasional stylistic nod to the Internet aesthetic – the use of Chicago as a headline type, standardized tags that lead the reader into each section – but these are misleading. Wow Wow is not a reflection of the Internet, or even

a review as its authors claim. It is a reworking; the editorial process successfully distils one system of information into quite another.

very straightforward, but the nature of Teller's photographs and the manner in which they have been edited belie the mechanics of the system. Effectively the book is a carefully constructed, fictional account of a successful fashion photographer's life – a late-1990's sequel to Michelangelo Antonioni's 1966 movie Blow-Up.

The GO-SEES system is a strange one – systematic disingenuity, possibly. To some extent, the first issue of Wow Wow[2], a magazine-format Internet review, edited and designed by MMS

(Fuel) in collaboration with journalist Richard Preston (a long-time collaborator with the group and author of Pure Fuel), relies on a similar device. MMS (Fuel) commissioned reviews of fifty-three Internet sites and then presented them consecutively, in an unhierarchical format. Divided into seven colour-coded categories, Wow Wow evokes feelings of an Internet that is both recognizable, but also utterly unfamiliar.
    Equality of information and

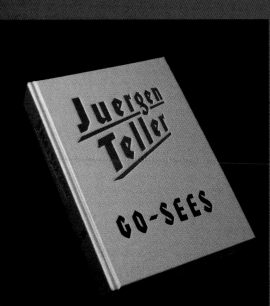

The cover of GO-SEES[1], a book containing photographs of models and aspirant models taken by Juergen Teller, is a witty composition. Set in red, custom-made, blackletter-style type, Teller's name recedes into the distance – the diminishing type size creates a trick of perspective that is emphasized by bold underscore. Beneath the name, the title appears in black capitals in the same font. Set against a gold background, the cover serves as a melodramatic entry to what is

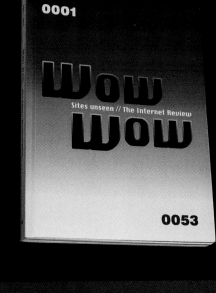

essentially quite a low-key set of images. There is something of *The Rocky Horror Picture Show* about the book – hundreds of fresh faces putting themselves in the hands of a stranger with a foreign accent. Actually, I don't know what Teller sounds like, but the cover of his book suggests a decidedly Germanic twang with perhaps a slight Transylvanian undertone.

Drawing on a questionable stereotype, this characterization of Teller is very appropriate – flicking

through the book's pages, it soon emerges that dubious stereotypes are the stuff of the publication. Co-conceived with Peter Miles of London design group Miles Murray Sorrell (Fuel) and designed by Miles with his partners Damon Murray and Stephen Sorrell, *GO-SEES* is a double-edged enterprise; the book feigns the identity of a dispassionate survey, but leaves no doubt that its disguise is knowingly transparent.

There is a system at work here. All photographs in the book were taken between May 1998 and April 1999. The images, each of a model or group of models standing at the entry to Teller's studio or in the street outside, are arranged chronologically. All the girls are named, except for the few whose names have been mislaid, and the date of their visit is recorded. The whole process seems

1. Teller, Juergen. *GO-SEES* (Scalo, 1999).

an apparently arbitrary emphasis on certain sections of text within each review – created by the use of various type sizes and colours – reflect the unsorted and sometimes confusing manner in which material arrives from the Web. Less like the Web, the magazine bubbles with content that the reader can access immediately without having to lumber through a series of elaborate hoops. MMS (Fuel) freely acknowledges the disparity between reading *Wow Wow* and

surfing the Web: the point of the enterprise was to turn the Internet into an open book, particularly aimed at latecomers to the medium and reluctant participants.

The choice of sites covered by the magazine was significant in creating disjunction between the Internet as we know it and the Internet as it is represented in *Wow Wow*. Concentrating largely on alternative culture, the magazine skirts the

2. Preston, Richard, ed. *Wow Wow* (London: Laurence King, 2000).

Wow Wow, 2000

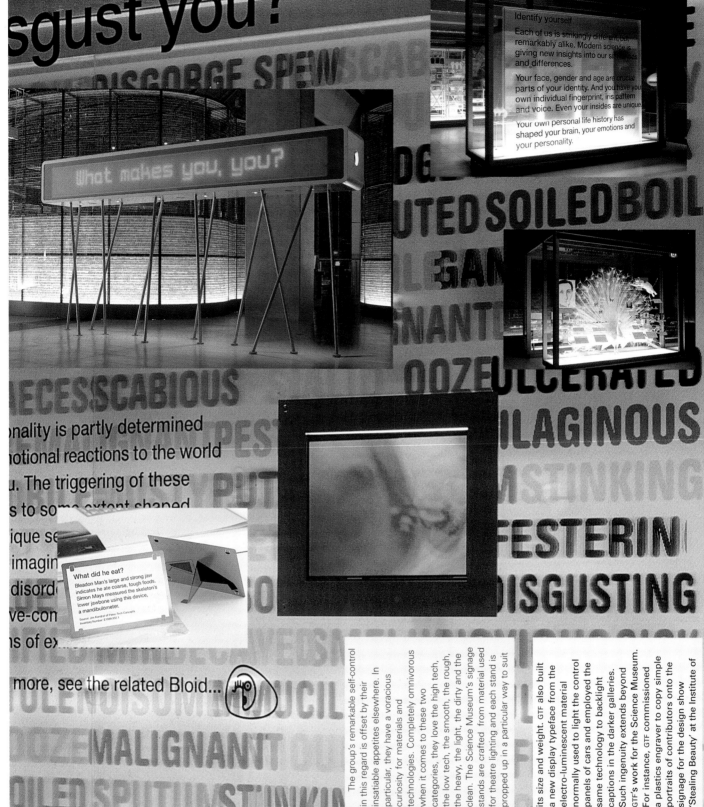

The visual expression of scientific principle is ridden with graphic clichés. Perhaps the most unshakable of these is the notion that Helvetica is the best typeface to convey scientific certainty. In their graphic design for two new galleries – 'Digitopolis' and 'Who Am I?' – at the Science Museum, the members of London-based Graphic Thought Facility (GTF) have faced the assumption head-on by choosing Helvetica for their exhibition captions. GTF's decision might seem

The group's remarkable self-control in this regard is offset by their insatiable appetites elsewhere. In particular, they have a voracious curiosity for materials and technologies. Completely omnivorous when it comes to these two categories, they love the high tech, the low tech, the smooth, the rough, the heavy, the light, the dirty and the clean. The Science Museum's signage stands are crafted from material used for theatre lighting and each stand is propped up in a particular way to suit

its size and weight. GTF also built a new display typeface from the electro-luminescent material normally used to light the control panels of cars and employed the same technology to backlight captions in the darker galleries. Such ingenuity extends beyond GTF's work for the Science Museum. For instance, GTF commissioned a plastics engraver to copy simple portraits of contributors onto the signage for the design show 'Stealing Beauty' at the Institute of

1/ THE COLOURS

Black is back as the interiors colour du jour. And not in its 1980s incarnation either. Where that was all about accessory sleek mattness, 21st Century black is glossy, lacquered and lustrous. Go matt on sheets, towels and curtains then add a flash of scarlet for bright relief — a single sofa, seat, cushion or cover will do. It's a powerful combination that speaks of confidence and positivity. Highlight with the merest smudge of pale blue or white.

2/ THE FURNITURE

Friends come to play, and stay. Hot dates turn into sweet sleepovers. What you need is flexible furniture... ROBIN DAY's SINGLE CV sofa, the EDINABOX, or a SIGMUND seat that stretches out and flips flat. Then eat well and socialise... in the round at ORBIT, a table in dark veneer, or go straight forward and simple on the modern oak RADIUS. Coordinate with oak basic benches, beds and drawers and don't overlook the details: rounded corners for that cosy cabin touch.

3/ THE TEXTURES

Create a place to dream in peace... swaddle in your comfort zone with unexpected texture. Put sheepskins, dyed black, red or left au naturel, underfoot as a treat for the toes. Laze away an afternoon on a fabulous felt flannel REVE daybed. And when evening draws in, pull closed velvet drapes, fetch your MORI lambswool throw and hunker down with a book on piles of fleece and mohair cushions. Or take to your bed, delicious in curl-up-able cotton and a SANSHO silk spread.

4/ THE LIGHTING

Change your world with light, at the flick of a switch. Whether task lights or mood lights, simple forms in modern materials work best. The CAPSULE lamp, glass shade and base in one, takes centre stage, acid etched or coloured black, white and blue. Alternatively keep a favourite shade but update it with a new base... perhaps white ceramic, lava stone black or beautiful blue and even bamboo. And for a little extra glitz and glamour... KEDY chrome spotlights.

5/ THE NEW NAMES

Tomorrow's talent today. RONAN BOUROULLEC... sophisticated, skinny, stackable tableware, the future shape of china. JULIE GOODWIN... also a ceramicist but her signature is jolly swoops of colour and a handmade vibe. GIOIA MELLER MARCOVICZ's SIGMUND sofa is the last word in flexible multi-functional furniture. Likewise LISA NORINDER's GROOVY sofa with attachable, detachable tabletop. ROSS MEUNEZ... the award winning New Yorker presents comfy COBBLESTONE cushions. And the equally celebrated AZUMIS add the simply brilliant EXX coatstand to Habitat's portfolio.

6/ THE OLD NAMES

20th Century Legends. ETTORE SOTTSASS.
As part of the Memphis design group, he railed against the pure functionalism of Modernism to laud liberation and provocation. Thus his Sottsass ashtray and vase for Habitat are almost too gorgeous for butts or blooms! SORI YANAGI. The legendary Japanese designer who assisted Charlotte Perriand, Le Corbusier's design partner, stays true to his Eastern roots with the YANAGI stool, so don't lounge, perch!

7/ THE PRODUCTS

Some things just define a season... the Vase. Full of flowers or even empty, a beautiful vase adds a precious point of colour to any room. Keep one for every season. BASE, BUD and FREEZE... perfect vessels in pale pink resin. In glass... CAZAL, warm and round like an amber gobstopper; DALMATIA, rotund or slender, graphic in black and white. And for purists: FERMOY, rectangular simplicity in dappled ceramic; RAITH, cylindrical in black ceramic; MANOLA, slim in white.

8/ THE FINISHING TOUCHES

Details make all the difference. Vietnamese lacquered CHI boxes. VITRINE mirrors. PIPE chrome containers. Even sheeny CANTON silk on sofas. The idea is... reflections where you least expect it, and smoothness where you want it. Shine... CHAIN PANEL curtains and Aluminium blinds. Indian soapstone for the bathroom, cork in the kitchen, silk in the bedroom. Surface finish, it's the final frontier.

For further information contact
Fiona Rushton / Berna Sermet at the Press Office:
Habitat, 196 Tottenham Court Rd, London W1P 9LD
Telephone 020 7255 6099 / 6067
Fax 020 7255 6001
E-mail press@habitat.co.uk
www.habitat.net

S BOND, THIS IS EDGY DARK AND MOODY; OR LE-FIN-DE-Y2K AND AT YOUR PLEASURE AND SEXY.

in white on a shiny black surface. GTF's treatment of Lubalin's typeface is significant. When Avant Garde was released in 1970, the wide-eyed optimistic futurism of the 1960s was already being replayed as a superficial decorative style. While Lubalin's typeface sits on the cusp between the earnest and the mannered, GTF's reworking of it pushes it decidedly over the edge on to the side of the lush. By making what was once ambiguous seem perfectly clear, GTF helped Habitat to package the feel of the early 1970s for uncomplicated contemporary consumption.

Leaflets and posters advertising designer Richard Paul Lohse's exhibition, 1999

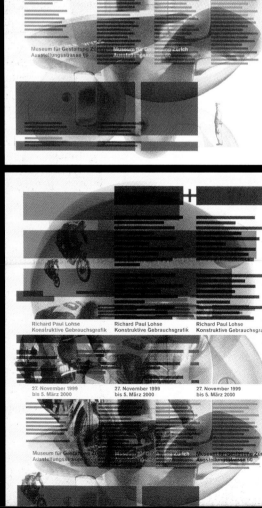
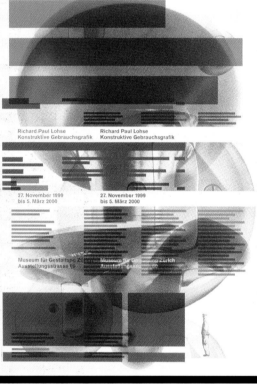
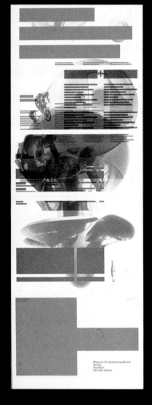

arrived simply printed in monocolour, by the end of the year it was delivered at the foot of a passage of colourful graphic texture.

Obscuring the text in this case was rational and easily justified. In other instances, Müller + Hess cross out printed words in a manner that, while no less systematic, cannot be explained in such straightforward terms. For example, in a series of designs for the magazine *Grenzwert* (published by the studio, pp.80–81), Müller + Hess repeat and overprint

Systems lie at the heart of design group Müller + Hess's working method. Rather than using their skills to tweak text and image in pursuit of perfect graphic form, the Zürich-based designers set up schemes whereby formal outcomes are determined automatically. They concentrate on devising robust rules and appropriate parameters and do not focus on the production of impeccable images.

Müller + Hess created a series of posters and leaflets to publicize an

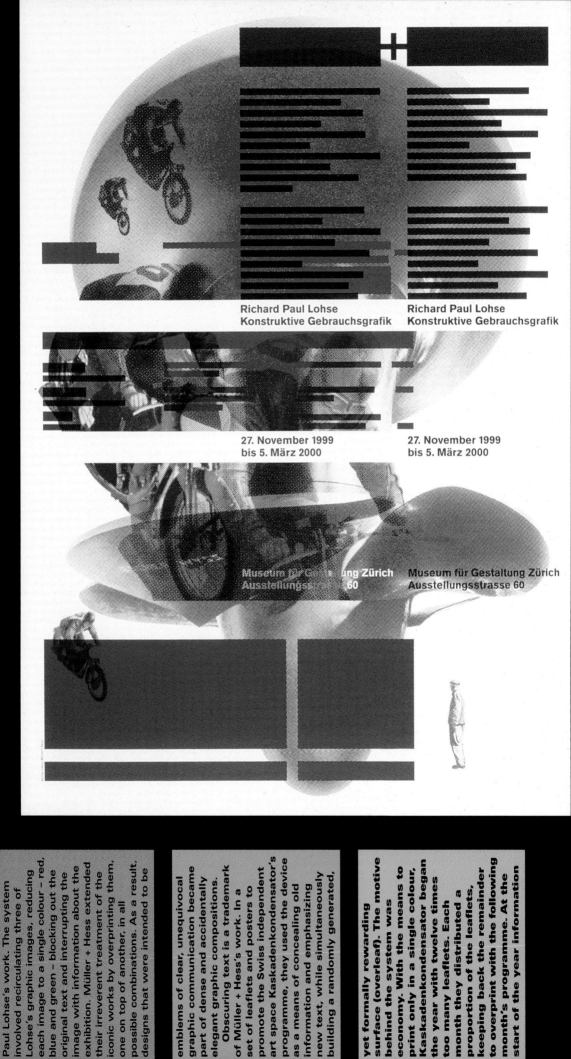

Richard Paul Lohse
Konstruktive Gebrauchsgrafik

Richard Paul Lohse
Konstruktive Gebrauchsgrafik

27. November 1999
bis 5. März 2000

27. November 1999
bis 5. März 2000

Museum für Gestaltung Zürich
Ausstellungsstrasse 60

Museum für Gestaltung Zürich
Ausstellungsstrasse 60

exhibition of Swiss designer Richard Paul Lohse's work. The system involved recirculating three of Lohse's graphic images, reducing each image to a single colour – red, blue and green – blocking out the original text and interrupting the image with information about the exhibition. Müller + Hess extended their irreverent treatment of the iconic works by overprinting them, one on top of another, in all possible combinations. As a result, designs that were intended to be

emblems of clear, unequivocal graphic communication became part of dense and accidentally elegant graphic compositions. Obscuring text is a trademark of Müller + Hess's work. In a set of leaflets and posters to promote the Swiss independent art space Kaskadenkondensator's programme, they used the device as a means of concealing old information and emphasizing new text, while simultaneously building a randomly generated,

yet formally rewarding surface (overleaf). The motive behind the system was economy. With the means to print only in a single colour, Kaskadenkondensator began the year with twelve times too many leaflets. Each month they distributed a proportion of the leaflets, keeping back the remainder to overprint with the following month's programme. At the start of the year information

[ALLES IN ORDNUNG?] Ein Projekt zum Thema Sammeln und Ordnen / 29.08.-30.11.97 >[TEIL 1]
>[1] GRUPPENAUSSTELLUNG 29.08.-14.09.97 / DANIELE BUETTI (Zürich) / MARKUS HÄBERLIN (Basel) /
BESSIE NAGER (Zürich-Brüssel) / DANIELA WETTSTEIN (Zürich) / Vernissage: 29.08.97,18h, Aktion von
Markus Häberlin / Werkgespräch: 11.09.97,19h >[2] DIE BEUTE DER JÄGER UND SAMMLER 05.09.97,19h /
Eine performative Berichterstattung / STEK AG-STEFAN KÄGI Künstler / REGULA J.KOPP Performance-
künstlerin / RAYELLE NIEMANN freie Kuratorin / VXNCI STIRNIMANN Feed Back & Forth (alle Zürich)
>[3] GEFÄSSE Kurzzeit-Veranstaltungen vom 19.09.-19.10.97 >[3.1] ÜBERALL IST VIEL 19./20./21.
09.97 / Video / ERIC HATTAN (Basel-Paris) / Werkgespräch:21.09.97,19h >[TEIL 2]

>[27.09.] SICHERES
WISSEN ALS MUSEUM, 19h, Vortrag: HINRICH SACHS, Künstler (Hamburg) / THE MISSING LINK, 20h, Ein
kriminologischer Vortrag: REINHARD STORZ, Kunsthistoriker (Basel) / TABELLEN, 21h, Vortrag:
REGINA IRMAN (Winterthur) / BEDTIME STORIES, 22h, Nocturne: Musik von Tom Johnson für Klarinette
Solo: JÜRG FREY (Aarau) >[28.09.] LOVATY, 20h, Konzert: Komposition für zwei Sprechstimmen von
Jürg Frey; HANS-JÜRG MEIER (Basel), PETER SONDEREGGER (Grellingen) >[03.10.] DAS GROSSE WEG-
WERFEN, 20h, Abend für Violine Solo: mit Werken von Bach, Streiff, Furrer-Münch, Baader-Nobs, Lovett,
Gubler, Zapf, Ayres: EGIDIUS STREIFF (Basel) >[04.10.] ONE HUNDRED THINGS, 20h, Vortrag: RICHARD
AYRES, Komponist (Amsterdam) >[05.10.] FILMABEND, in Zusammenarbeit mit Neuem Kino, 20h: BERLIN,
DIE SINFONIE DER GROSSTADT (D,1927) von WALTER RUTTMANN / AMENIC (CH,1993) von BEAT BROGLE /
ZWEI FIGUREN, ROT & BLAU (CH,1995) von ESTHER HIEPLER / BLINDNIS (CH,1994) von MATTHIAS CADUFF
>[10./11./12.10.] SONDERAUSWAHL/MANGELWARE (KONSERVIERUNG 5), Präsentation: VERA BOURGEOIS
(Frankfurt) / Vernissage: 10.10.,18h / Performancegespräch: 10.10.,19h >[17./18./19.10.] BEBEN IV,
Präsentation: Seinsmographische Sammlung, hier: weiblich; KAREN SCHOLZ (Köln) / Vortrag und Ge-
spräch: 19.10.,19h >[4] EINZELAUSSTELLUNGEN >[24.10.-9.11.] MEHR ODER WENIGER, Serielle Arbeiten:
VERENA THÜRKAUF (Basel) / Vernissage: 24.10.,18h / Werkgespräch: 07.11.,19h >[14.11.-30.11.] GAÇON
SCHAFFT ORDNUNG: VERSION X, Installation: CLAUDE GAÇON (Basel) / Vernissage: 14.11.,18h / Werkge-
spräch: 27.11.,19h >[27.11.] ALLES IN ORDNUNG?, 19h, Roundtable (Werkgespräch Gaçon): CLAUDE
GAÇON, Künstler (Basel) / MATTHIAS HALDEMANN, Kunsthistoriker (Kunsthaus Zug) / DANIEL HÄNI, Kul-
turraumschaffender (Basel) / MAYA RIKLI, Künstlerin (Kaskadenkondensator) / REINHARD STORZ, Kunsthistoriker (Basel)

KASKADENKONDENSATOR Warteck pp Burgweg 7 4058 Basel Tram Nr.2 bis Wettsteinplatz
Forum für zeitgenössische Kunst und Musik / Dokumentationsstelle für Basler KünstlerInnen, in den Bereichen bildende Kunst, Architektur
und Video. Öffnungszeiten: Fr-Sa / 16-19Uhr (wenn nicht anders vermerkt) oder nach Vereinbarung T 061 693 38 37

Der Kaskadenkondensator wird unterstützt von: Bundesamt für Kultur / Kulturpauschale Kanton Basel-Stadt / Ernst Göhner Stiftung, Zug /
Migros Kulturprozent / Schweizerische National-Versicherungs-Gesellschaft, Basel / Stiftung für kulturelle, soziale und humanitäre
Experimente, Binningen / Stiftung Birsig für Kunst und Kultur, Basel / Technische Unterstützung: Schreinerei Schwarz n'Egger, Basel /
Druckvorlagen: Bader Repro AG, Münchenstein / Druck: Druckerei Cratander AG, Basel / Siebdruck: Arni, Allschwil
Müller+Hess

KASKADENKONDENSATOR Warteck pp Burgweg 7 4058 Basel Tram Nr.2 bis Wettsteinplatz
Forum für zeitgenössische Kunst und Musik / Dokumentationsstelle für Basler KünstlerInnen, in den Bereichen bildende Kunst, Architektur
und Video. Öffnungszeiten: Fr-Sa / 16-19Uhr (wenn nicht anders vermerkt) oder nach Vereinbarung T 061 693 38 37

Der Kaskadenkondensator wird unterstützt von: Bundesamt für Kultur / Kulturpauschale Kanton Basel-Stadt / Ernst Göhner Stiftung, Zug /
Migros Kulturprozent / Schweizerische National-Versicherungs-Gesellschaft, Basel / Stiftung für kulturelle, soziale und humanitäre
Experimente, Binningen / Stiftung Birsig für Kunst und Kultur, Basel / Technische Unterstützung: Schreinerei Schwarz n'Egger, Basel /
Druckvorlagen: Bader Repro AG, Münchenstein / Druck: Druckerei Cratander AG, Basel / Siebdruck: Arni, Allschwil
Müller+Hess

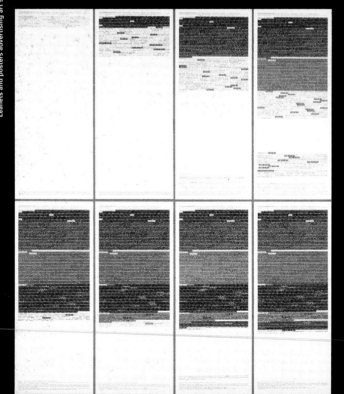

text and images to arrive eventually
at a set of difficult and aggressive
surfaces. In typography, the act of
making letterforms illegible is always
highly charged. Absolutely contrary
to prescribed typographic practice,
maybe its only meaning is derived
from its iconoclasm.

Common to all the systems
activated by Müller + Hess is an
understanding of the printing
process and the will to generate
maximum effect through economic
means. As with all attempts at

[>[27.09.] ... [28.09.] ... >[03.10.] ... >[04.10.] ... >[05.10.] ... >[10./11./12.10.] ... >[17./18./19.10.] ... >[24.10.-9.11.] ... >[14.11.-30.11.] ... >[27.11.]]

[NONLIEUX] Poesie des Nicht-Ortes. Das Projekt findet hauptsächlich im [öffentlichen] Raum statt / 24.01.-22.03.98 >[TEIL1] >[24.01.] Kaskadenkondensator 16h: SILVIA BUOL: ORTE ANKREIDEN (Bewegungsperformance) / ab 17h: DANIELA KEISER: THE STREET CLOSE TO THE PARKING* (Internet) / MIRIAM STEINHAUSER: WORLD WIDE BODY* (Internetprojekt von MISS) / CHRIS ZUFFEREY: Bildbetrachtung* / STUDER.V.D.BERG: BAS3L* (Stadtplan) / SIMON BAUR: Intervenierender Kurator* / >[24.01.] Warteck Turmstübli 17h: PETER REGLI: REALITY HACKING 133 (Installation bis 28.02.) / >[24.01.] dynAthletik-Center, Riehenstr.167 ab 18.30h: THOMAS HIRSCHHORN: OTTO FREUNDLICH-ALTAR (Strassendenkmal bis 07.02.). Apéro an der Erfrischungsbar im dynAthletik-Center / >[24.01.] McDonalds, Rosentalstr.71 20h: SUSANNA BRANDLI: MENU SURPRISE (dîner performatif, Anmeldung bis 20.01. unter Tel. 031/311 10 26) / >[30.01.] Kaskadenkondensator 19h: JEAN MARIE CLARKE: O'ZONE STATION 1993-2000 (Installation mit Performance bis 13.03.) / ab 20h: AGATHA ZOBRIST und THERBS WAECKERLIN: DIESSEITS UND JENSEITS* (Intervention) / >[31.01.] Elsässerstr.5-9 ab 14h: CRISTA ZIEGLER (Fotoinstallation)* / >[31.01.] Hammerstr.123 16h: MARTINA SIEGWOLF, mit BETTINA STUCKY: KLEINBASEL MITTE (Stadtsicht) / ab 20h: BAR INSTANT CLUB / >[14.02.] Verkehrsinsel, Falknerstr. Hauptpost 15-17h: ANNE HODY und ALBAN RÜDISÜHLI: KEIMFREI (Performance) / >[15.02.] Kaskadenkondensator ab 15.30h: TACHEMAGOS: MOMENTART*IMMA (Dokumentation) / 16h: GERTRUDE MOSER-WAGNER: INDICATORE (Videoprojektion, bis 22.02.) / 17.30h: CHRISTOF RUSCH: NICHT-ORTE, NOCH-NICHT-ORTE, NICHT-MEHR-ORTE IN UND UM ROM (Sightseeing in Wort und Bild) / MAX MATTER: Vortrag / anschliessend ROUNDTABLE, Gesprächsleitung FRANZISKA BAETCKE / >[21.02.] Drahtzugstr.48 ab 14h: RENATE BUSER: DRAHTZUGSTR.48* (Fotoinstallation) / >[21.02.] Ort siehe Tagespresse ab 15h: SERGE HASENBÜHLER: NONLIEUX-NONIDENTITE* (Fotoinstallation) / >[21.02.] unterwegs TACHEMAGOS: MOMENTART*IMMA (Aktion) / >[21.02.] Ort siehe Tagespresse ab 20h: BAR INSTANT CLUB >[TEIL 2]

>[17.04.-10.05.] ... >[10.05.] ... >[17.05.]
[LISTE 98 - THE YOUNG ART FAIR] >[10.06.-14.06.] 13-21h: Kaskadenkondensator präsentiert sich gemeinsam mit HOTEL (Zürich) / KIOSK (Bern) / KONSUMBÄCKEREI (Solothurn) / KUNSTRAUM AARAU (Aarau) / Vernissage: 09.06., 16-22h

would-be utilitarian graphic work, their output begs the question of whether the utilitarianism is authentic or merely aesthetic pose. No design process allows the designer to completely disregard formal issues, but, that said, the work of Müller + Hess employs certain methods that qualify as being genuinely functional. Unlike previous generations of graphic designers who, in the guise of utility, offered grandiose, overarching graphic solutions,

Müller + Hess suggest no more than ad-hoc, workable graphic proposals. The differences between old-style and new-style utility are typified by the studio's approach to grid-based typography. Whereas the old school demanded that text be squeezed into the perfect grid, the new school allows text to unfold messily within the grid structure. Content is contained by Müller + Hess's graphic systems, not confined.

KASKADENKONDENSATOR | Warteck pp | Burgweg 7 | 4058 Basel | Tram Nr. 2 bis Wettsteinplatz |
>1 VERONIQUE ZUSSAU | BLANC COMME NEIGE | 12.10.-03.11.96 | Vernissage:11.10.96,19Uhr | Werkgespräch:01.11.96,19Uhr | >2 ARIANE EPARS | INS BLAUE HINEIN | 16.11.-08.12.96 | Vernissage:15.11.96,18Uhr | >3 POUR LE CLAVIER | JEAN-JACQUES DÜNKI (Klavier, Clavichord) in eigenen Werken | Matinée | So 24.11.96,11Uhr | >4 SUSANNE FANKHAUSER | 14.12.96-05.01.97 | Vernissage:13.12.96,18Uhr | Werkgespräch: Do 19.12.96,19Uhr, ab 16Uhr geöffnet | geschlossen:23.12.96-02.01.97 | >5 HEINRICH LÜBER | DOWNLOAD | Performance | 14.01.97,18-21Uhr | >6 ERNST THOMA | INSTANT SOUND NETWORK | Konzert | Do 16.01.97,20.30Uhr | >7 PASCALE GRAU / SIMONE KURZ / ANDREA SAEMANN | LEIBLIED VARIATIONEN | ... >8 SIBYLLE HAUERT UND MUDA MATHIS | THE PLOT, DIE VERSCHWÖRUNG, HEY MARY JANE, WHERE ARE YOU GOING WITH THIS SCISSORS IN YOUR HAND | 22.02.-16.03.97.10-21Uhr | Vernissage:21.02.97,19Uhr | Werkgespräch:14.03.97,19Uhr | >9 CHRISTOPH BÜCHEL | ZU VERMIETEN | 05.04.-20.04.97, Do-So 16-21Uhr | Vernissage:04.04.97,18Uhr | >10 CHIARENZA & HAUSER & CROPTIER | HEUTE IST ES ÜBERALL SCHÖN | 02.05.-25.05.97 | Vernissage und CD-Taufe:02.05.97, 19Uhr | Kunst und Öffentlichkeit. Thematisches Werkgespräch mit Philip Ursprung (Zürich) und Gästen:23.05.97, 19Uhr |

Der Kaskadenkondensator wird unterstützt von: Migros Kulturprozent | Schweizerische National-Versicherungs-Gesellschaft, Basel | Stiftung (für kulturelle, soziale und humanitäre Experimente, Binningen) | Öffnungszeiten: Fr-So | 16-19Uhr | (wenn nicht anders vermerkt) | oder nach Vereinbarung | T 061 693 26 40 | >3 | T 061 692 94 51 | >4 | T 061 322 19 26 | >5/6/7 | T 061 381 39 12 | >8 | T 061 691 89 24 | >9 | T 061 261 89 72 | >10 | T 061 261 89 72 |

Chair, video sketch, 1999

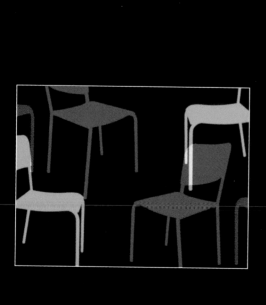

The chair that stars in this sketch is
Anthony Burrill's and, like so many
of the motifs in Burrill's work, it has
an exaggeratedly generic quality.
London-based Plowman and Burrill
took twelve photographs of the chair
at different moments of rotation,
then animated the images in a series
of minimal, twelve-frame cycles.
As the chair rotates on the screen,
it multiplies and takes on the basic
colours from which all TV pictures
are built: red, blue and green. The
turning chairs overlap and their

various colours combine to create
the full spectrum of TV hues (red
+ blue = magenta, blue + green =
cyan, red + green = yellow and red
+ blue + green = white). The result
is a simple sequence that explores
television's most fundamental
properties.

The soundtrack for this sequence of motion graphics is from an interview with Phil Oakey: 'What we have got in this is not simple, like everything else, it's not even complex, it's multiplex'. The background image is a photograph from the amateur archive (that documents the construction of London's M25 motorway) of Paul Plowman's uncle and aunt. Both dating from the early 1980s, words (spoken in Oakey's distinctive nasal tone) and image combine to create an otherworldly

complex

flatness that belies the apparent
insistence on multiplicity.
Over the course of the
sequence, Multiplex's typographic
identity arrives on the screen in
four parts and coheres at its
centre. Although it is a piece of
three-dimensional typography,
it makes no attempt at any real
sense of perspective and instead
lies flat upon the screen, in keeping
with the tone of the words and
images it overlays. There is an
irony here. Plowman plays with

the notion that the ideas and
projects that seem the most
complex and forward-thinking
for their time are also those that
date most quickly, a phenomenon
that dogs television in particular.
Constantly striving for the new,
TV sequences seem clunky and
inept almost immediately after
their release. Effectively
the Multiplex sequence acts
as a celebration of the rusty
residues left behind by the
progressive urge.

At the cusp of a
broadcasting revolution,
the exact nature of which
remains obscure to most
of us, Multiplex's simple
televisual experiment is
rather poignant. A significant
part of our
childhoods, TV has had the
ability to press nostalgia
buttons more effectively than
any other medium. Multiplex
offers a visual hymn to a
longstanding companion.

\<Vulture Reality\>

Macro Meals
Men Only
Wall Fans of India
sub urban
9 by 5
Oscillocity

Jake Tilson

video compilation

hannahsleeps
Jake Tilson

Jake Tilson

Hungerford
Bridge
tide and trains

Vulture Reality, video compilation, 1991–99
Hannahsleeps and *Hungerford Bridge Tide and Trains*, audio cassettes, 1998–99
Pearl Street, CD, 2001

JAKE TILSON   CITY SOUNDS of the EVERYDAY 15

PEARL STREET at 4 am

nightclub and roadworks • New York City

DURATION > 17 minutes 24 seconds

recorded in New York City from a third floor
apartment on Pearl Street at Broad Street
at four o'clock in the morning.

AUDIO CD   ATLAS

The most focused of all Tilson's demonstrations of the particular and the generic is a sixty-minute recording of his daughter's somnolent breaths entitled *Hannahsleeps* (1998). Bordering on the sentimental, Hannah's sweet snufflings are redolent of the common experience of parenthood; the birth of a child submerges the new parent into a set of totally ordinary, but nonetheless overwhelming, feelings of love and anxiety.

Jake Tilson (London) travels the world in search of the unremarkable. Eschewing images of well-known tourist attractions – the visual clichés in most photo albums and home videos – Tilson concentrates on pictures of cheap meals and urban traffic. If he were to found 'Tilson Tours', Jake Tilson would titillate jaded global tourists with extravagant round trips through the strangely familiar.

Tilson's focus veers away from the centre of a spectacle and fixes

firmly on its edges. In the video *sub urban* (1993–96), the railway tracks of Paris, Bombay and Tokyo run in parallel in three vertical screen segments. From this viewpoint, the three cities become almost indistinguishable; the fabric of each urban centre is the common by-product of international capitalism. Against a background of such uniformity, famous landmarks seem like theme-park attractions grafted on top of urban mulch with the

intention of maintaining the fiction of international variation. Running against such a pessimistic interpretation, other of Tilson's short films celebrate the survival of the particular over the generic. A survey of India's wall fans (1993–96) draws attention to the plethora of variation in the mechanics and location of rotating blades. In a similar vein, although not as palatable, a collection of images of men's urinals in India and

Japan hints at significant differences in the practice of hygiene across classes and cultures. Tilson's most extended study of cultural difference is the film *Macro Meals* (1991–96), video images of forty-five meals taken across the globe over the course of five years. *Macro Meals* reveals the extremities of the international catering industry, exploring chips in three continents.

Jake Tilson

Video stills from *sub urban*, *Men Only*, *Wall Fans of India* and *Macro Meals*, all appearing on the *Vulture Reality* compilation, 1991–99

'The Cooker', website, 1994–2001 [this page]. 'Tell-Tale Signs', website, 1999 [opposite]

Indio Swap Meet Arabia and Doctor Carrion Blvd. Indio CA
Sablon market Brussels
Annex Antiques Fair & Flea Market 25th St & 6th Avenue New York City
Marché aux Puces de Montreuil Paris

Jake Tilson

'Invisible Exports', commissioned project for *Restart*, 2000

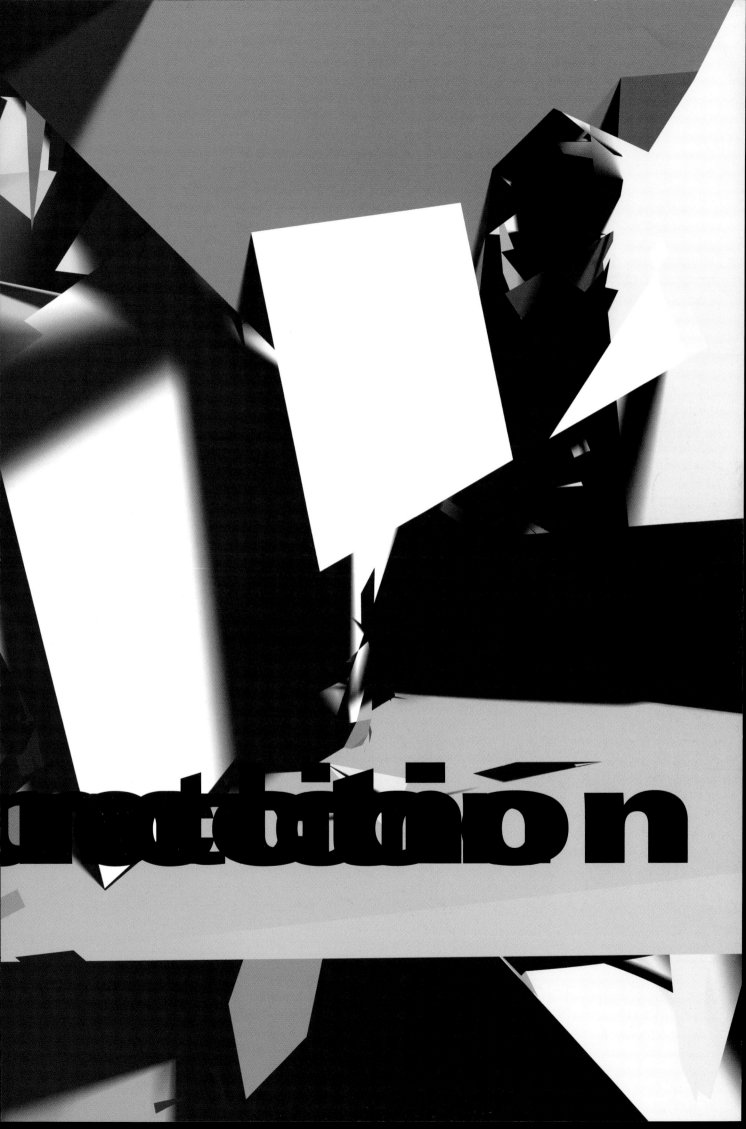

Not unified by an alliance to a particular formal style, the work presented in this chapter is drawn together by the will to systematically complicate and provoke, to challenge and to question. Alongside emotionally mute, code-driven compositions sits the extravagant theatrical work of such graphic designers as London-based Peter Saville and Paris design team M/M. Catalyzed by disjuncture, Saville's work exemplifies yet another multidisciplinary approach: the desire

Konstantin Grcic has pursued the theme of balance by designing mass-produced metal-and-wood shelving systems that stand off-centre and wobble. His designs are understated, but they abrade the assumptions at the core of his industry. Artist Adam Chodzko threw audiences off balance in his two-part artwork *Better Scenery*. He raised two signs, one in the car park of a North London shopping centre and the other in a desert in Arizona; each sign describes the whereabouts of the other. Chodzko's

works along similar lines to Chodzko's signs. Over a series of three images Hyland establishes a forlorn and disturbing mini-narrative through the mismatch of word and image.

Thematic Intersection
In Restart I sketch out themes, but do not describe boxes. Much of the graphic work relates to the issues that have been raised, but none of the designs can be contained by words. Many of the projects here could be located in the intersection

between these themes. For example, Mevis + van Deursen's work concerns ideas about code and about generic design; Scott King's Crash project employs everyday design – the visual language of desktop publishing – to produce disjunctive effects; 2x4's work with Rem Koolhaas/OMA aims to throw users pleasantly off balance by employing the codes of information design in a series of unexpected contexts. Over the course of the book, I hope that graphic systems have been given a chance to create a space of their own.

to simultaneously chafe and seduce. A characteristic of the well-honed techniques of surrealism, this desire is an identifiable undercurrent in the work of many contemporary designers and artists. In a similar vein, M/M have collaborated with photographers Inez van Lamsweerde and Craig McDean to plumb glutinous photographic depths, emerging with a series of rich yet disturbing images. The tendency to titillate and torture

is evident beyond graphic design. Shoe designer Adele Clarke has a collection called 'Off Register', in which shoes unbalance their wearer out of line. It is footwear that challenges fashion's idea of the female form yet remains glamourous. Other artists and designers have used disjunction to produce equally vertiginous but less theatrical (and less sexual) effects. Product designer

signs have been constructed using a range of visual languages from supermarket signage to traditional conceptual art. All the languages are used with intent and meaning, but none of them are quite at ease, creating a sense of discomfort and in turn questioning how we perceive and describe our sense of place. London-based graphic designer Angus Hyland created a piece for the 'Ultravision' exhibition in London that

Building: McCormick Tribune Campus Center
Architecture: Rem Koolhaas/OMA, Rotterdam
Graphic Design: 2x4, New York

A new student center on the campus of the Illinois Institute of Technology designed by the Office for Metropolitan Architecture. The IIT campus was designed, famously, by Mies van der Rohe after the second world war. The new building will occupy a long abandoned site beneath the elevated railway tracks. A giant sound-baffling tube, enclosing the train tracks, will allow the space below to be reclaimed. Except for the auditorium/ballroom and the bar, the entire building is one story, organized in a flat "Pompeian carpet of program". The graphic design system includes navigational devices, signage, directories and large-scale images that wrap wall and window surfaces.

Proposal for IIT campus centre (in collaboration with Rem Koolhaas/OMA), 2000

working with Koolhaas on commissioning an enormous photographic mural that will wrap the building, on designing embroidered curtains that will shield the auditorium and on the conception of an ambitious signage and navigational system that will appear through the building to deliver specific and ambiguous information.

The entrance to the proposed campus centre is through a pair of glass doors set within an eight-metre-high (twenty-six feet) portrait of Mies

van der Rohe. Entering through Mies's chin, the user will realize that the image is made from symbols drawn from the signage system. The aim of rendering Mies's face in the elfin figures and playful icons is to use the emblems of high modernism in fresh, unexpected ways. 'Mies, THE towering figure of 20th-century architecture' notes Rock 'becomes literally towering.'

The proposed designs for the IIT campus centre are works in progress, all ideas being discussed

While the campus has doubled in size over the last forty years, the number of students attending the Illinois Institute of Technology has diminished. Architect Rem Koolhaas's proposed campus centre addresses the problem directly. Through the simulation of population density, Koolhaas (of Office for Metropolitan Architecture, New York) hopes to encourage an actual density sufficient to foster social activities.

The original buildings of the IIT

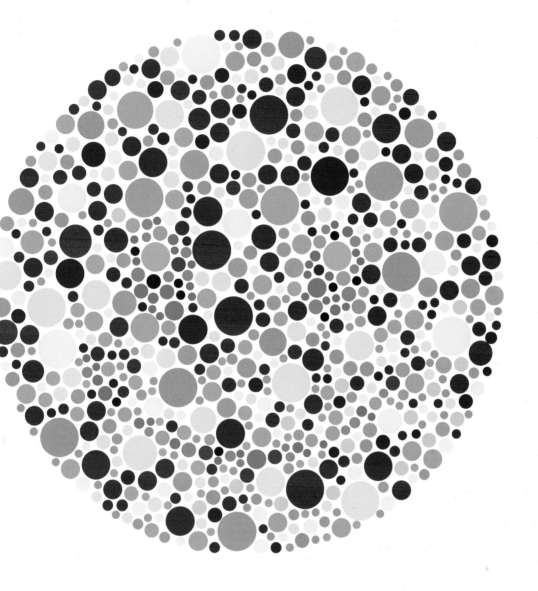

Graphic-design system and stained-glass window for IIT campus centre, 2000

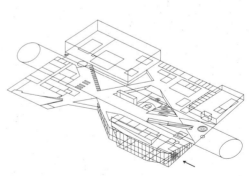

by Koolhaas and 2x4 remain flexible and subject to change. Already established, however, is a benchmark for architectural and graphic interaction.

were designed by Ludwig Mies van der Rohe and to be successful any addition must relate to the venerated structures. Koolhaas has sited his building directly under the elevated train tracks that cut through the campus, rendering a formerly dead space usable by encasing the tracks in a soundproof tube. Koolhaas's plan is inspired by the structure of Pompeii, a city that predates town planning and offers frozen evidence of spontaneous urban swarm. In

effect two very disparate models are forced together: cool Miesian rationalism and chaotic unplanned urbanism. The intention is to create an exciting combination that will in turn lead to unforeseen interactions.

The façade and interior surfaces of Koolhaas's campus centre are colourful and communicative. This is where New York-based 2x4 comes on the scene. Working with

Koolhaas, they are helping to design a building that will not simply speak, but will shout, laugh and sing. A large stained-glass window of circular glass panels depicts a smiley face to set the tone. To paraphrase 2x4's Michael Rock, the building is about 'institutionalized, officially supported FUN'. The studio's involvement extends to every corner of the building. Aside from the window, they are

Mies van der Rohe entrance to IIT campus centre, 2000

Symbols used to compose Mies van der Rohe entrance façade for IIT campus centre, 2000

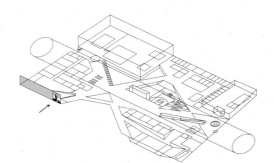

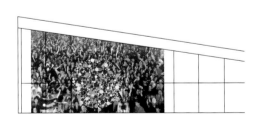

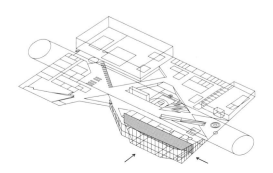

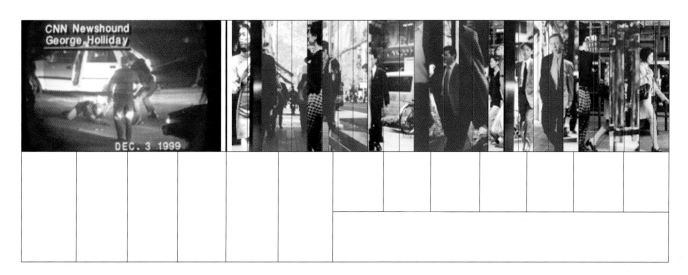

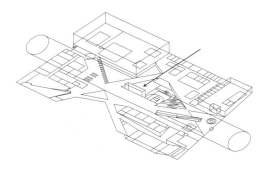

Commissioned project for *Restart*, 2001

Alexander Boxill's collaboration with photographers is ongoing, open-ended and experimental. Rather than a method of representation, photography is part of a process of representation to the designers – the photographic surface is a starting point and a determinant of the final image.

The images are an unlikely inventory of London-based Alexander Boxill's recent work. They were made by exposing the pair's latest projects – books, leaflets and

catalogues – directly onto colour photographic paper and then reworking the results in PhotoShop. Besides being a record of their work, the images have a spectral quality, a technicolour immateriality. This is not the first time that Alexander and Boxill have turned objects into shadows of themselves. Working with photographer Andrew Penketh they experimented repeatedly with such techniques as exposure and x-ray – techniques that have the

dual and contradictory effect of recording material existence while rendering the subject ghostly.

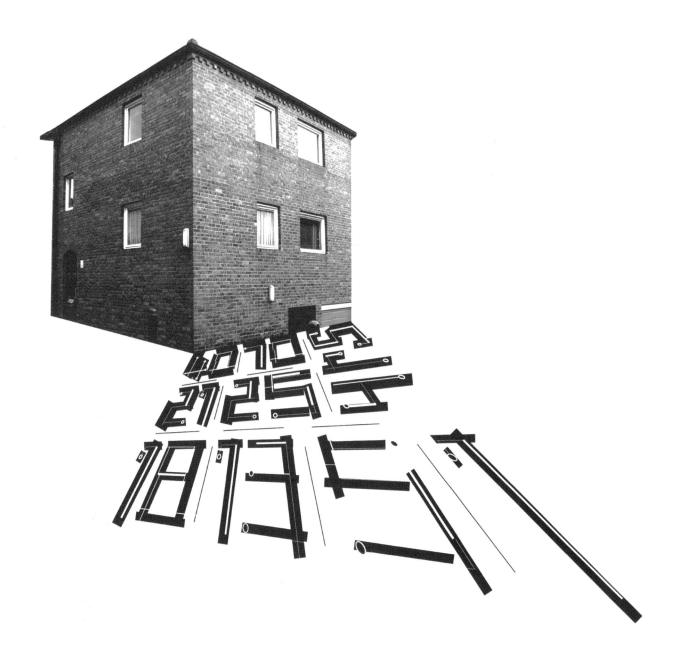

graphic surface on which information
is reduced to pattern.
    Anderson uses information as
associative rather than for its precision.
The value of that approach hinges
on the audience's willingness to
participate in the exercise – and their
ability to make those associations.

Peter Anderson (whose studio is
in London, but who often works
in Northern Ireland) uses part of
his creative energy on information
maps, imaginary territories that
are the outcome of fusing and
reworking various sets of data.
In the first and second 'Northern
Ireland' series, the maps explore
the relationship between territory,
history and identity.
    The first 'Northern Ireland' series
Transglobal Numerals shows a set
of images that merge in and out

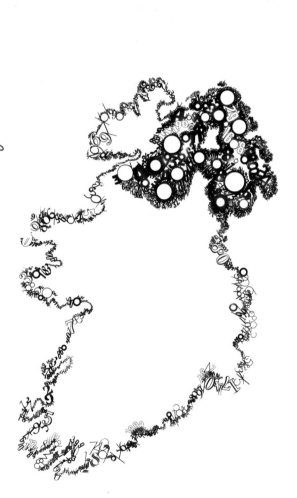

of one another on a lightbox. Anderson proposed three associations between time and place: 'Landscape' forms an outline of Ireland from important dates in Irish history (confounding the expectation that it must be a record of 'the troubles', all dates mark positive events); 'Incident' presents a fluid chain woven from the exact times of these events; and 'Character' plots the boundaries of a domestic garden with the significant ages of an

ordinary life. In series, these images move the viewer through political to personal information and back again.

Anderson's second 'Northern Ireland' series was designed as installations and printed material for the Belfast restaurant Cayenne. In *Moving Surnames*, Anderson collected every surname in the Northern Ireland telephone directory and placed them at random within a rejigged Belfast street map. The result is

a set of unexpected juxtapositions between people and places – a politically charged gesture in the context of unresolved questions about territory and identity. Less overtly political and also part of the second series, in *Does Living in a Valley Make You Curious?*, Anderson drapes layers of geographical data over a computer-generated landscape to create a dense

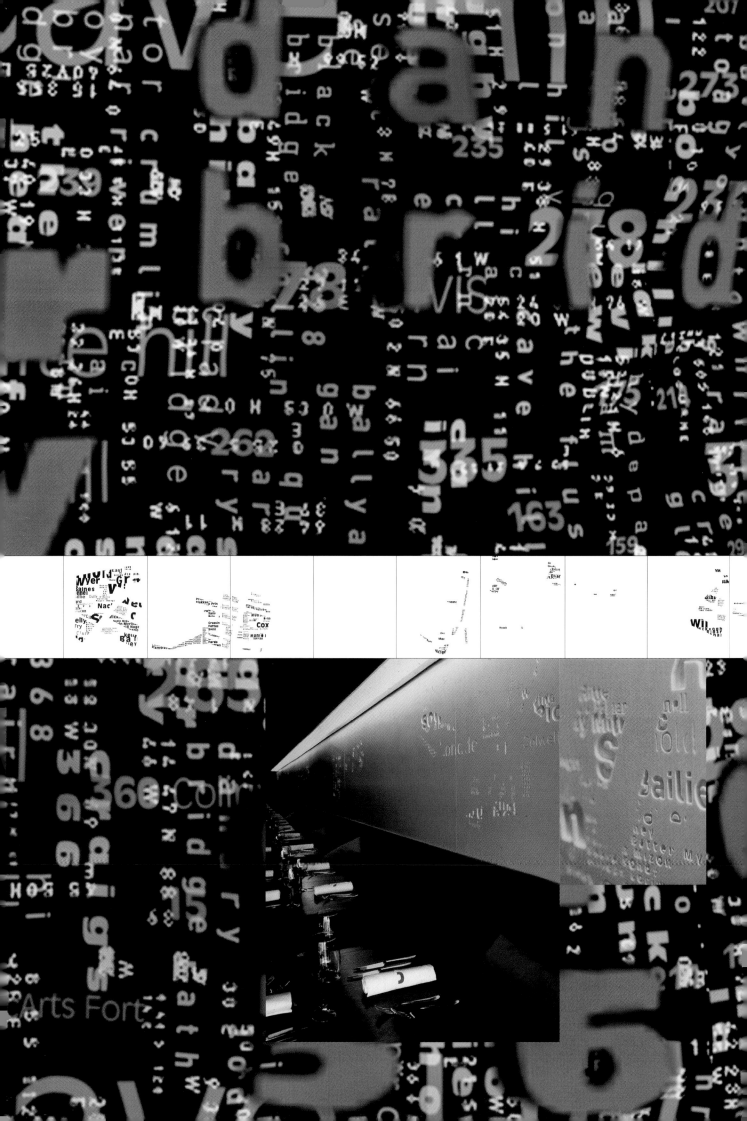

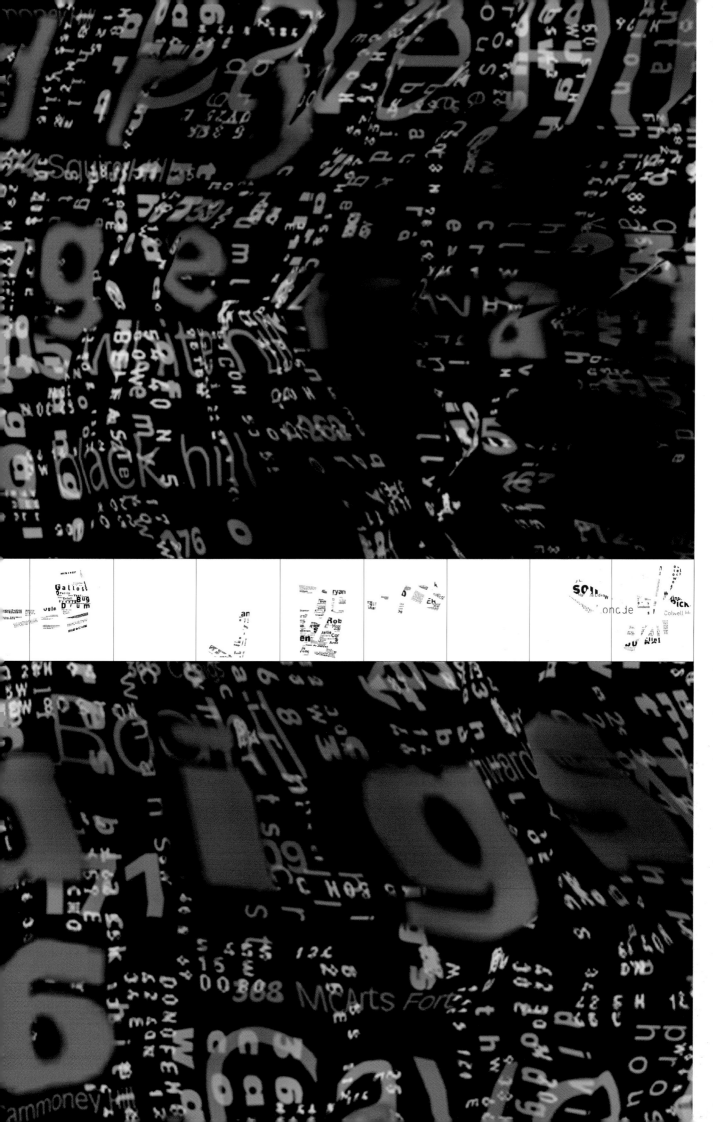

Peter Anderson

Moving Surnames and *Does Living in a Valley Make You Curious?* (second 'Northern Ireland' series), installations for Cayenne restaurant, 1999

109

Workspirit Six, book for Vitra, 1998 [this page]
Think Book, corporate history for SHV, 1996 [opposite]

Around the end of the 1980s, people's conception of the working environment began to change. New technologies and evolving social structures seemed to destroy the rationale behind conventional office organization, and a series of alternative working practices – hot-desking, working from home, flexitime – became big news. On its introduction, each method appeared to be successful, but now the future seems certain to be one of diffuse but interconnected ways of working.

In 1991 Irma Boom and art historian Johan Pijnappel were commissioned to construct a commemorative corporate history for Dutch firm SHV's centenary in 1996, which would be distributed exclusively to company shareholders and key staff. *Think Book*'s purpose was to demonstrate what those in the company called the 'SHV mentality', and to focus on 'the most salient examples of this mentality over the past 200 years' (the mentality apparently predating the company, which runs fuel and cash-and-carry outlets).

Boom and Pijnappel began by listing key words that not only described SHV's thinking, but also established the designers' ideals and interests. Unafraid of bringing their own perspective to the project, the designers emphasized that over five years a strong personal involvement would prove essential. The list meant that SHV, Boom and Pijnappel committed themselves to forming a dedicated, low-key, kind and forward-looking team.

Having established their position,

appear on the cover or the opening pages; instead, it is revealed letter by letter over the course of the volume. Other cohesive devices include: a series of questions that set the tone of the enquiry 'Can man think beyond his own thought?', 'What can we say without eyes?'; the use of watermarked paper, which hints at events beneath the surface of established history; and the overlaying of one kind of information with another, a graphic element that demonstrates the complexity of the historical course.

The freedom, time and money offered to Boom and Pijnappel by SHV in the production of Think Book is unprecedented, and graphic exercises of this nature are very unlikely to become commonplace. Although sceptics may doubt the motives of the company (is this no more than a very extreme form of self-aggrandizement?), the book does justify itself. It is a very satisfying object and the account it gives of the company is thorough, straightforward and often irreverent.

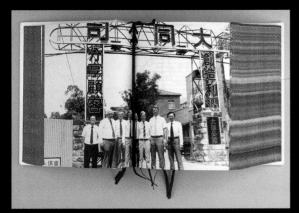

Irma Boom's book *Workspirit Six* for furniture manufacturer Vitra explores the new world of work. The spaces portrayed in the book may be uniformly idealized, but they are highly diverse. Flicking between conference-, court- and living rooms, the reader is invited to link scenarios through the use of spyholes that have been cut from the page. Effectively the book is an illustration of diffusion and interconnectivity. The circle motif on the cover and at the edge

the designers buried themselves deep in the company's archive. Over the following five years they pieced together a weighty history that intertwined corporate, political and familial events; placed alongside one another in the book are company documents, business ephemera, family photographs and images of historical incidents. Disparate elements were woven into a single account through a feat of editing and design. Beginning with the then present (1996), Boom and

of the pages emphasizes the idea of patterns emerging through the assembly of scattered elements.

Vitra is known for the quality of its print promotions (Boom was introduced to Vitra chairman Rolf Fehlbaum by Tibor Kalman, the designer of two previous *Workspirit* publications) and *Workspirit Six* is part of a very broad marketing effort. Boom (Amsterdam) enjoyed the opportunity to collaborate with Vitra's marketing department

Pijnappel moved back in time through the story of SHV. Although it is impossible to digest in one session, the book is engagingly paced and delivers satisfying segments of specific historical information and a general feeling of the period.

The visual diversity of the material is unified by Boom in a series of bold design interventions that thread through the book's pages. For example, the title does not

and addressed the task of communicating the company's message in earnest. Vitra's distinctive office furniture is visible throughout the book, and placed alongside it are lists of words and phrases compiled by Boom to convey the corporation's arena and its ideals. Breathtakingly positive, the book describes a universe to which we can all aspire.

Paint Removing Exercise, installation at the Royal College of Art, Henry Moore Gallery, 2000 [this page]
Titanic – A Typographical Account of a Journey to the Bottom of the Sea, 1995 [opposite]

PAINT REMOVING EXERCISE

Royal College of Art Entrance Gallery 17 January 2000
Polythene Dust Sheet 6m²

INSTRUCTIONS
Equipment required: Sponge, flat scraper, wire brush, sand paper
Protect all immovable furnishings, electric's and flooring with supplied polythene dust sheet
Remove all emulsion

Soak painted surface with water | Remove all dampened paint with flat scraper | Scrub patches of excess paint, using wire brush | Remove fragments of paint, using water and scraper | Remove uneven surfaces with coarse sandpaper

Use an alternative to Vinyl Emulsion paint such as specialist environmental paints (available mail-order) from Auro (01799 5848888) and Livos (01952 883288)

HARMFUL

BRILLIANT WHITE VINYL EMULSION

1. Contains Volatile Organic Compounds (VOCs). These compounds are substances which evaporate from petroleum solvent paints. Asthma, Allergies and Sick Building Syndrome (with flu-like symptoms) are caused or worsened by the release of VOCs.[1]

2. VOCs are considered to be the reason for decorators' risk of lung cancer being increased by 40%.[2]

3. Vinyl emulsions continue to 'offgas' VOCs for a considerable time after application.[3]

4. VOCs emissions contribute to smog and low level ozone formation which, amongst other things, can injure plants and contribute to global warming.[4]

5. Production and manufacture of vinyl emulsion paint in the UK creates 55,000 tonnes of VOCs pollution per year, nearly as much as road vehicles (65,000 tonnes per annum).[5]

6. The production of 1 tone of Vinyl Emulsion can result in up to 30 tonnes of waste.[6]

7. The Vinyl referred to is Polyvinyl Acetate. A Swedish study of Polyvinyl Acetate production found that 40% of workers had some form of occupational skin disease.[7]

8. The biocides and other ingredients in Vinyl Emulsion paints can be serious water pollutants if it enters the drains through brush washing or disposal.[8]

9. The pigment Titanium Dioxide (TiO²) is added to provide opacity. It accounts for the majority of the energy consumed in production and it causes water pollution, respiratory problems, skin irritation.[9]

10. The main impacts of paint manufacture are the high energy processes required and the use of (non-renewable) crude oil as the raw material. The Petroleum Industry generally is a major source of greenhouse gases and acid deposition, and is responsible for over half of all emissions of toxics to the environment.[10]

Brilliant White Vinyl Emulsion was produced in the UK for **Johnstones Jonmat / Leyland Paints.**
Manufactured by **Kalon Decorative Products, Huddersfield Road, Batley, West Yorkshire W1F7.**

Kalon Group is a company of
Total, Tour Total, 24 cours, Michelet, La Defense, 10, F-92800 Puteaux, France.

Total is involved in twenty oppressive regimes, including a joint venture with the repressive military regime to build a pipeline across Burma to Thailand. Apparently, thousands of indigenous people have been relocated and forced by the military to clear forest and build roads and railways for pipelines. There are also allegations of torture, rape and murder at the hands of the regime. Aung San Suu Kyi, leader of the democratically elected government prevented by the military from taking power, has described Total as 'the strongest supporter of the Burmese military.'[11] Total's taxes paid to Burma's military regime amount to approximately US $200 million.[12] A boycott of Total was called by the Methodist Church in June 1998 over Total's investment in Burma and France's nuclear testing.[13] Total's US $1 Billion gas pipeline, which runs from an offshore gas field overland to Thailand was reported that slave and child labour was used during building of the pipeline.[14] Total had 4 oil spills in 1996, taken into account when oil is released in production the total amount of oil released by Total was 86.5 tonnes. More recently the Empress Tanker leaked 72,000 tonnes of Total's desiel oil on the West coast of France. The desiel oil spread over 300 miles of coast line, killing 300,000 varieties of sealife and birds. The incident has been described as an economical disaster for the local communities.[15]

References 1. Building for a Future, Winter 1998 2. Simply Build Green, John Talbot (Findhorn Press, 1995) 3. Eco-Renovation, Edward Harland, Green Books 1998 4. Paint the Room Green, Environmental Building News, February 1999 5. Simply Build Green, John Talbot (Findhorn Press, 1995) 6. Ethical Consumer April/May 1999 7. Simply Build Green, John Talbot (Findhorn Press, 1995) 8. Ethical Consumer April/May 1999 9. Greener Building – Products and Services Directory, AECB 1998 10. The Global Environment, Two Decades of Challenge, MK Tolba 11. Down to Earth, International Campaign for Ecological Justice in Indonesia May 1997 12. Corporate Watch, from Reuters 13 November 1996 14. Financial Times 28 November 1995 15. Corporate Watch, John Pilger, December 1999 16. Royal College of Art Prospectus 99/00

The Royal College of Art gratefully acknowledges the substantial help and support it receives from sponsors Leyland Paints.[16]

Concept and Communication by Darren Hughes 00.01.17

Allotted a space in a student show at the Royal College of Art in London, Darren Hughes chose to scrape the paint off the walls. Working energetically – until he was stopped by a member of the college's staff – Hughes caught the shards of emulsion on a polythene dust sheet that was printed with advice and information on the technique and purpose of paint removal.

A first-year MA student at the time (and now with a studio in London),

ship sinks. Information surrounding the diagrams records the drift of the two halves, the ship's geographical position and the depth reached by the wreckage. Over eight prints, the u-shapes become increasingly large as the wreckage nears the sea bed. Noting the exact time of each stage of the catastrophe, Hughes heads the prints with a brief, step-by-step account of the facts.

The film makes one wonder whether it is acceptable to graft narratives upon real events, reinventing memories and taking them out of the hands of the victims and their families. Although very different in approach, Hughes's prints raise a similar question – just what is an appropriate response to history's sorrier tales?

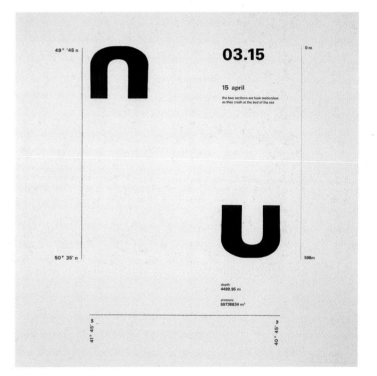

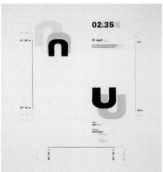

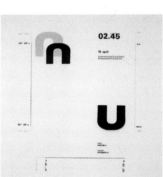

Hughes had been disturbed to learn that the Royal College of Art accepted sponsorship from Leyland Paints, part of the multinational corporation Total. Listing allegations against Total, taken from such sources as *Ethical Consumer* magazine, Hughes hoped to raise pertinent questions about the practice of commercial sponsorship in the college.

In the context of the gleaming white galleries of the RCA, the project has particular resonance.

It is college policy to present student work as professionally as possible to promote the seamless placing of graduates in the commercial realm. Chip away at the smooth, public façade and you mount an attack on the core values of the institution.

In James Cameron's 1997 film *Titanic*, information about the tragedy was sensationalized to become part of a predictable love story. Conversely, Darren Hughes's letterpress project,

Titanic – a Typographical Account of a Journey to the Bottom of the Sea, synthesizes several accounts of the disaster to produce a cool, diagrammatic description of the incident.

Hughes's prints relay the train of events from a viewpoint at the bottom of the sea. Initially represented by a rectangle, *The Titanic* then splits into two u-shapes that float further apart as the

Untitled, contribution to 'Ultravision' exhibition at British Council (interior of exhibition room, below), 1999

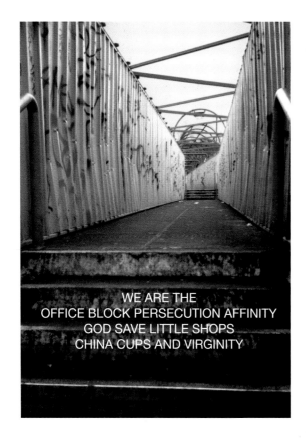

WE ARE THE
OFFICE BLOCK PERSECUTION AFFINITY
GOD SAVE LITTLE SHOPS
CHINA CUPS AND VIRGINITY

WE ARE THE
VILLAGE GREEN PRESERVATION SOCIETY
GOD SAVE STRAWBERRY JAM
AND ALL THE DIFFERENT VARIETIES

The rebranding of Britain, a project associated with the 1997 election of a Labour government after a long period of Conservative rule, was always going to be a spurious affair. The government's plans to turn the country around using nothing but PR gloss were met with almost universal scepticism.

Taking part in the 1999 'Ultravision' exhibition, Angus Hyland (London) confronted the rebranding issue head-on. Using three sequentially merging images,

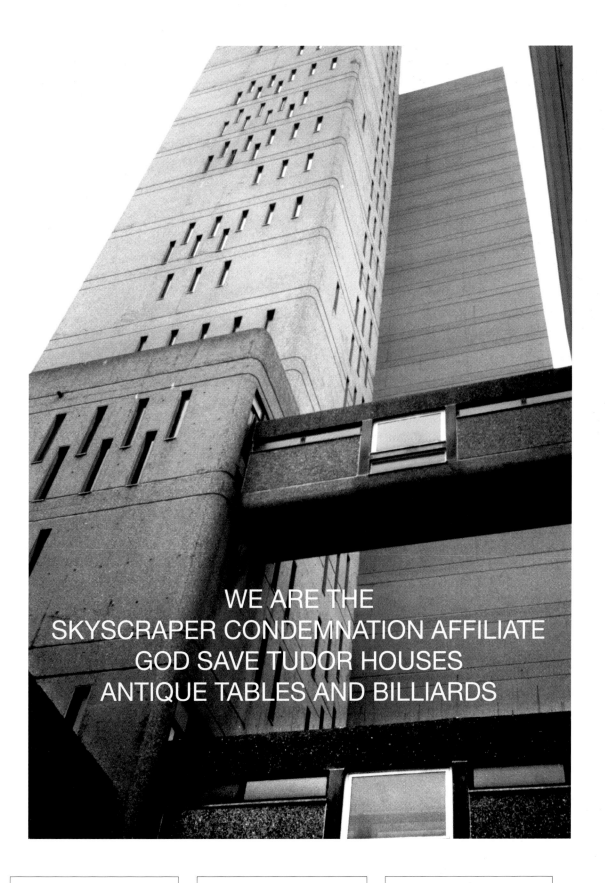

WE ARE THE
SKYSCRAPER CONDEMNATION AFFILIATE
GOD SAVE TUDOR HOUSES
ANTIQUE TABLES AND BILLIARDS

Hyland projected a view of Britain that was utterly opposed to anything the Labour spin doctors might have promoted. Hyland superimposed a lyric written by Ray Davies of The Kinks over photographs of the shabby urban remains of British modernism. The words from the song 'The Village Green Preservation Society' are the rhetoric of an imagined band of Little England vigilantes, a group that is prepared to use drastic

methods in defence of a traditional way of life. Hyland's Britain is one of uncomfortable extremes, but although his vision is bleak, his intentions are not doctrinaire: his aim is simply to offer a corrective to those who hope to wish away society's sharp edges.

However distressed London's Notting Hill may appear in Hyland's shots, soaring house prices have rendered what remains of its tattiness a

piquant emblem of urban authenticity. The tower block in the third image – Trellick Tower – has now been recast as a modish residence, meaning that, ironically, the rebranders may have triumphed (although it is money, not PR flannel, that has effected the transformation).

Kurt Cobain, detail from 'Into the Black', 2000 [left]
Meanwhile In A large Central London Apartment ...., 1999 [right]
Photographs advertising 'Crash' exhibition at the ICA, London, 1999

KURT COBAIN WAS BORN
IN SEATTLE

HE WAS THE SINGER AND
GUITARIST IN THE POP
GROUP *NIRVANA*

THEY MADE RECORDINGS
FOR DAVID GEFFEN

THESE RECORDINGS WERE
PRESSED ONTO A VARIETY
OF PLASTICS AND SOLD IN
THEIR MILLIONS AROUND
THE WORLD

ON 8TH APRIL 1994 COBAIN
TOOK A SHOTGUN AND
BLEW HIS OWN HEAD OFF

AT HIS HOME IN SEATTLE

Meanwhile In A Large Central London Apartment The Telephone Is Ringing...

Tamara Beckwith: Hi, me speaking.

Ulrike Meinhof: Good afternoon. My name is Ulrike, I'm campaigning for the Red Army Faction.

Tamara: Sorry. Who?

Ulrike: I'm from the R.A.F.

Tamara: Cool. Great guys, bombed the Nazis.

Ulrike: That's correct. So, you will make a donation towards the struggle against bourgeois consumer capitalism?

Tamara: Look Ulrika, I'll happily make a donation, providing I get invited to do more 'Shooting Stars'.

Ulrike: That's perfect. Shooting stars is high on our agenda, along with bombing bureaucrats and killing cops. Do you have any further requirements?

Tamara: Well...I have to be on Mark's side.

Ulrike: Good. I too am on Marx's side.

Tamara: You are? So who's on the other side?

Ulrike: The whole might of Western Capitalism.

Tamara: Well, that's hardly fair.

a staple of new-school subversives, who are happy to trade in the contradictions of early-twenty-first-century existence.

Crash, the irregularly published anti-style magazine/pamphlet/fanzine produced by London-based Scott King in collaboration with writer Matthew Worley, is remarkable for its mismatched editorial and typographic styles. King's design is flat and strangely unemphatic while Worley's writing is an extended, vicious rant. *Crash* adopts a tone of sour disgust, and Worley reserves special vitriol for the media: the class war is recast as the people's fight against TV (and *Hello* magazine).

Photography by Jonathan de Villiers

In a demonstration of the public's relationship with the media, King has interpreted certain well-remembered live-music events as a set of top-heavy fractions (overleaf). With the dots below the line representing members of the band (in this case, The Sex Pistols) and those above signifying the audience, the inequality of the association becomes evident. The diagrams are an illustration of the gulf between being one of the few

and one of the many.

In contrast with the disorienting empty typography of the magazine, the photographic images are highly staged and very slick. Art-directed by King and photographed by Jonathan de Villiers, the illustrations employ the well-honed skills of experienced advertising and fashion stylists to alternative ends. Many of the photographs offer seductive yet nasty visual puns. Their impact relies on the

difference between the smooth surface of the photographic set-up and the brutality of the subject. One outcome is that protest becomes inextricably bound with what is being protested against. This technique would have seemed highly problematic to old-style revolutionaries, who sought untainted modes of expression, but has become

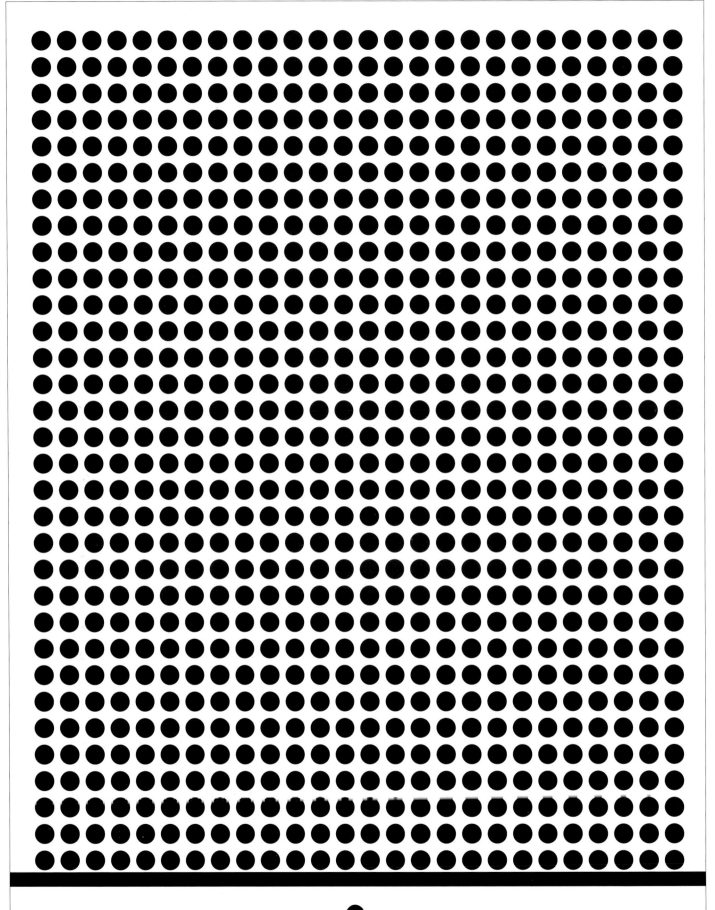

Sex Pistols, 14 January 1978, Winterland, San Francisco, U.S.A.

Sex Pistols, 6 July 1976, 100 Club, Oxford Street, London.

Paul was just one of those lads: The best clothes, the prettiest girlfriend, the best fighter. It was even rumoured that in sixth form, he shagged Miss Clark, the French teacher.

Peter and Paul's mums are best friends, they went to school together. Peter's dad and Paul's dad have had to learn how to be friends. It wasn't easy because Paul's dad used to go out with Peter's mum. The fact that both Peter and Paul had football trials for their county seemed to help both dads find a way to 'let bygones be bygones'. But it's pretty superficial, because Peter's dad openly 'has his doubts' about Paul.

Peter's mother regularly points out that her son is 'The Spitting Image Of Marti Pellow'. While Paul's mum often declares that 'Girl's Think The Sun Shines Out Of Our Paul's Arse'.

For as long as anyone can remember Peter and Paul have been mates. They even share a house.

'Soap Opera'. Photography by Jonathan de Villiers

Meanwhile, In The Nelson Mandela Bar...

Jon: Che is still an icon, an inspiration to revolutionaries worldwide. A hero to those of us who understand that self empowerment only arises from direct action; and that direct action is the only viable weapon against capitalist oppression. Wouldn't you agree comrade?

Will: You're right...comrade...as a singular iconic force within the western world, Cher remains supreme. A true spiritual leader, whose vision has never been surpassed. Not even by Madonna.

Jon: The Lady Madonna is an archaic symbol of repression, a shrine to populist paranoia. People follow her in fear of expressing their own opinions. Worship as an attempt to suppress the collective will of the masses.

Will: Madonna is the ultimate symbol of manufactured mediocrity. Her vacuous reign over the hearts and minds of the weak has been achieved by what can only be understood as blatantly manufactured...corporate...fascism.

Jon: You're right. I can see that you truly understand how the modern icon is usually created comrade. However, I would argue that Che has now surpassed the simplistic status of a consumable icon. Comrade, I am thinking 'saint'.

Will: I am thinking 'angel'.

Jon: Absolutely. Remember what Che said? 'Man really attains the state of complete humanity when he produces, without being forced by physical need to sell himself as commodity'.

Will: Yes, and Cher has stuck by that maxim to the letter. Cher had achieved more than most of us ever will by the age of twenty five, but the will was strong, the message had to be spread. Of course you remember what Cher also said: 'I'm walking in Memphis walking, walking in Memphis. But do I really feel the way I feel?'

Jon: It's clear what the sub-text is there. One can only read that as Che subtly ridiculing the inherent moral poverty of American imperialism. 'Walking' being a metaphor for isolation, a hopeless yearning for purpose within the oppressive capitalist machine.

Will: At last, I have finally found a kindred spirit. Can I get you another drink...comrade?

Scott King

Soap Opera, 2000 [opposite]
Front and back of *Cher Guevara poster*, 2001 [this page]

Issey Miyake's 'Pleats Please' collection, 1997

Mitsuo Katsui (Tokyo) was one of the first Japanese designers to apply computer technology to graphic design. In the early years of the process (the late 1960s and early 1970s), computers were unwieldy and inefficient, and the contrast between these unappealing hulks of technology and the slick and seductive surfaces coaxed from them by Katsui is striking. Computer technology has advanced a great deal, but the disconcerting beauty of Katsui's designs still seems

elfinlight
K series

graphic by mitsuo katsui

PLEATS
PLEASE

ISSEY MIYAKE

something of a miracle.
    Applied to dresses in Issey
Miyake's 'Pleats Please' collection,
Katsui's graphic texture creates
garments suitable for unearthly
creatures (elves, apparently).
Encased in shimmering rivers
of colour the body loses its
straightforward physical
dimensions and becomes
something more indeterminate,
more atmospheric.

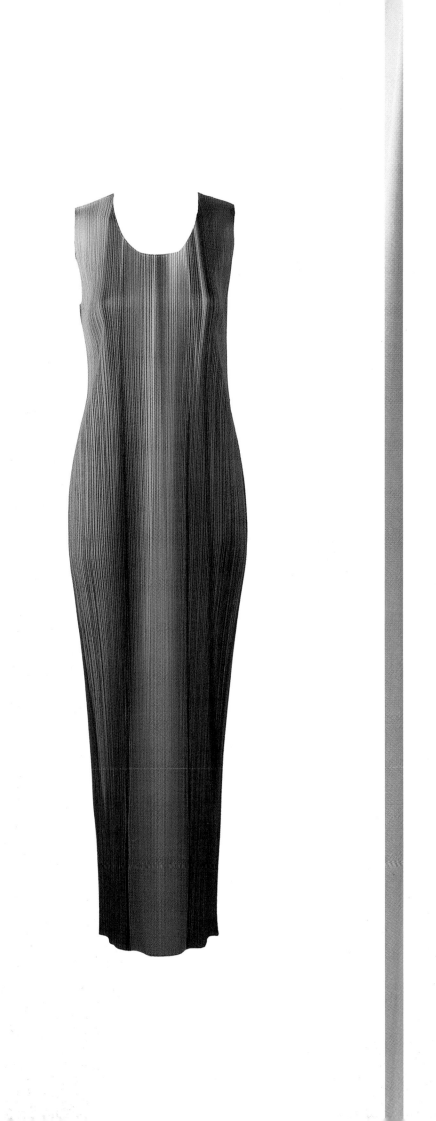

MATSURI ● design:mitsuo katsui. operation:kentaro ota. produced by jagda. 1999

Dresses from Issey Miyake's 'Pleats Please' collection, 1997

Mitsuo Katsui

In Spring/Summer 1999 (overleaf) M/M and M/M began a new chapter in their work. The season's catalogue is a dark essay on marriage in which a male and female model appear adorned and bound by elaborate nuptial garments. M/M drew freely over M/M's photographs, both decorating and obliterating the original image. As in previous catalogues, the relationship between the compositions and psychoanalytic thought is unmistakable; by dressing in wedding clothes a person asserts their identity as part

of a couple, but negates their identity as an individual.

M/M have worked with Craig McDean on the Fall/Winter 2000/2001 catalogue, which is in a very different mood to M/M's earlier collaborations with M/M. Although still story-led, the catalogue is a great deal more extrovert, looking beyond the darkness of the inner being. Model Amber Valetta poses in front of a series of large-scale photographs of America. Wrapped in quilted clothes and fur, she has

M/M (Paris) does not offer clients a short-lived problem/solution design experience, rather the studio hopes to draw them into meaningful, long-term, creative relationships. The fruits of the courtships are evident across M/M's output, but are perhaps best illustrated by the catalogues designed for Yohji Yamamoto since 1995. Yamamoto's relationship with M/M is purposefully indulgent; the fashion designer delivers the clothing and then stands back to allow M/M to determine the

Yohji Yamamoto's Fall/Winter 2000/2001 catalogue

POST NO BILLS

imagery. Over the course of five years the studio has worked with a range of photographers – David Sims, Paolo Roversi, Inez van Lamsweerde & Vinoodh Matadin and Craig McDean – to construct an evolving and increasingly distinctive art direction.

The point of no return for M/M and Yamamoto – the moment when the catalogues departed emphatically from mainstream fashion imagery to follow a trajectory of their own – occurred

something of the pioneer about her. In some images Valetta tentatively puts on a tissue-paper Halloween mask; her uncertain relationship with the object lends her the appearance of an explorer uncovering the customs of a strange new world.

M/M's Yamamoto catalogues have a quality that is rare in the world of fashion: they combine modish immediacy with the ability to deliver much more over time. Between 1997 and 2000 the

when the graphic designers commissioned Inez van Lamsweerde & Vinoodh Matadin to photograph the Spring/ Summer 1998 catalogue. M/M and IVL/VM used a set of simple props to create an unsettling atmosphere with unmistakable psychoanalytic overtones. The outcome is a surrealist fairy tale; a strange world where objects have obvious emblematic properties yet their scale and character change from scene to

Centre Pompidou in Paris, which houses France's national collection of modern art, underwent a major millennial refurbishment and was closed to the public while its galleries, libraries, public spaces, offices and storerooms were reorganized and refitted. At the same time, M/M teamed up with curator Fabrice Hergott to produce a catalogue that would present the collection in a new light, and which was published

scene. In the follow-up catalogue, Fall/Winter 1998/1999, the team drenched a forest clearing in a pool of artificial light and furnished it with a set of ambiguously two- and three-dimensional forms. A model interacted with the objects in a manner that was by turns malign and defeated to create imagery redolent of witchcraft, weird yet accessible.

Yohji Yamamoto's Spring/Summer 1999 catalogue

on the reopening of the centre at the beginning of January 2000.

After acquainting themselves thoroughly with the centre's archives, the designers worked with the Pompidou's curatorial team to distil the collection from forty-thousand objects to 521 images. The images – mostly pictures taken directly from the archives, augmented with some newly commissioned photography of the museum's books and documents – were arranged in the catalogue in a predominantly, but not dogmatically,

chronological sequence. This allowed the collection to tell a fresh story and in particular removed the burden, traditionally placed on the objects of modern art, of illustrating the last century's great art-isms. With captions and extraneous information kept to a minimum, pictures are intended to spark off one another rather than fall in line with an overbearing art-historical construct.

Overall, MM's publication (XXe/MNAM/Collections: Une histoire matérielle) looks fairly

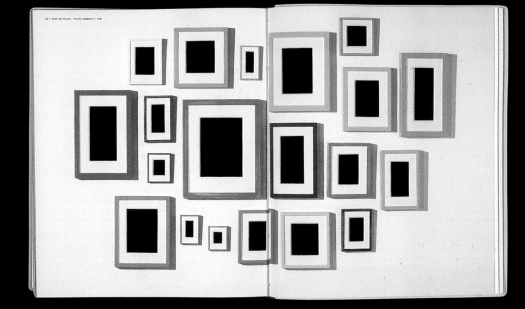

stark – wipe-clean grey plastic covers, full-bleed images, minimal text. To off-set this restraint, M/M used a striking typeface, designed specifically for the project, which created an elaborate, neo-art-nouveau texture. It was constructed from a minimal repertoire of simple forms and the occasional, unconstrained flourish of illustration. Although the catalogue reveals the Pompidou collection's weaknesses along with its strengths, the publication has

generally been received as being open-ended and exhilarating, a contrast with the rehang of the centre's galleries, which have been widely deemed pedestrian and overdetermined.

XXe/MNAM/Collections: Une histoire matérielle, catalogue for the Centre Georges Pompidou, 2000

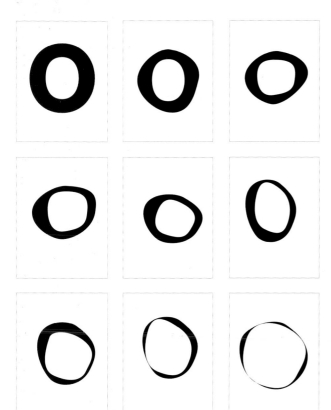

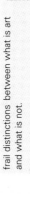

frail distinctions between what is art
and what is not.

Bruce Mau (Toronto, Canada) created
an identity for VOID, a now defunct
industrial design office (the name
may have proved too much of a
temptation to fate), that is built from
a set of seven imperfect ovals in
a muted colour spectrum. Layered
concentrically, one on top of the
other, they form a ragged o-shape.
As a metaphor for the practice
of industrial design, the identity
suggests that the pursuit of
technological improvement does not
preclude humanity and idiosyncrasy.

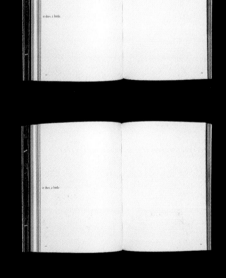

The collaboration between
Douglas Gordon and Bruce Mau on
a book to accompany the 'Douglas
Gordon • Black Spot' exhibition
has generated a few myths.
Supposedly the pair pampered
and tempted their inner muses –
a process involving champagne,
oysters and pedicures – to discover
a means of surmounting any
barriers that might exist between
art and design, emerging with
a publication that is engaging from
every perspective.

As a virgin object, the book
seems to be a solid black box,
an impression created by black-
edged paper. On the front and
back covers are Gordon's initials
set in 666-point white type.
The coded representation of
the beast – 666 – is a restrained
intimation of evil and is
characteristic of the entire
publication. Turning the pages,
an extraordinary combination
of the overwrought and the
understated is predominant.

Primarily a record of
Gordon's text-based work,
the illustrations are largely
typographic. Gordon and
Mau have created an
autobiographical introductory
essay purely from pictures,
thereby inverting the usual
order of an art catalogue –
an art readership expects
to have to wade through text
before being rewarded by
image. Such a radical move
presses fearlessly on the

On/Off, limited-edition rotogravure, 1999

way that bricks are units of architectural construction. They also raise questions over the relationship between book-making and the book itself. To create the bricks, J. Abbott Miller used all the essential processes of book-making (binding, trimming, drilling, embossing) except for printing. As a result the brick books lack what is most important to books: ink on paper. Therefore, the position of the brick books in the gallery is ambiguous; they are stand-ins (self-professed liars, even) that have been marshalled in poetic defence of the real thing.

As gallery exhibits, Miller's brick books were stacked into a series of follies; as art commodities they were signed, numbered and sold one by one. Conceived in response to an invitation to show at the Andrea Rosen Gallery in New York, the project is a rare example of design being granted the cultural and commercial privileges assumed by fine art.

A rotogravure is a photographic print made by exposing an object or image through a lens and prism so that its reversed impression is thrown upon light-sensitive paper. The resulting prints have inky, black depths and fine, expressive lines. For New York-based Ellen Lupton and J. Abbott Miller, rotogravure became a means of translating pristine, digitally composed images into two, rich, materially emphatic, 14-x-22-inch, limited-edition prints entitled *On/Off*.

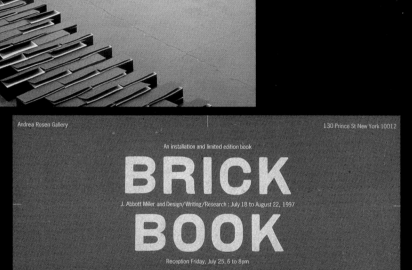

Andrea Rosen Gallery   130 Prince St New York 10012

An installation and limited edition book

BRICK
BOOK

J. Abbott Miller and Design/Writing/Research : July 18 to August 22, 1997

Reception Friday, July 25, 6 to 8pm

tel: 212 941 0203   fax: 212 941 0327

Lupton and Miller were invited to make *On/Off* by Graphicstudio, a print workshop at the University of South Florida that has been renowned for its work with artists over the last thirty years. The prints explore the representation of light on paper in the darkness-defined medium of gravure, and the designers are producing a publication that continues the investigation using traditional offset printing. The experiments are part of a larger, ongoing project

on luminous typography – a follow-up to Miller's previous work on dimensional typography.

Apart from being an adventure in light and darkness, Lupton and Miller's prints make a basic point about digital technology: either it's on or it's off. Spelling the word 'On' in beams of light and 'Off' in their absence, the designers are employing an off-screen medium to express the fundamental conditions of on-screen typography.

J. Abbott Miller's brick books are the same size as the American brick and are drilled with the same three characteristic holes. Each of their edges are painted by hand so that, placed alongside one another, they create the visual texture of an ordinary brick wall.

The presentation of the brick books' suggests that books are units of knowledge within a library in the same

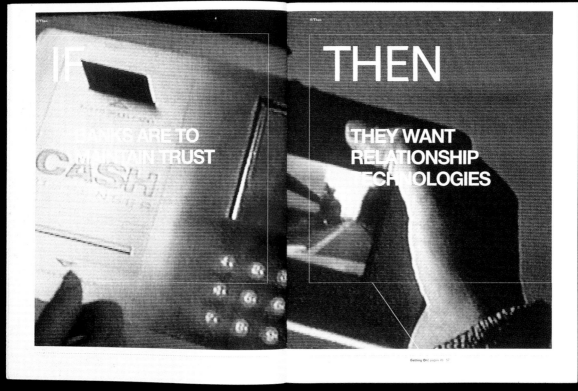

IF THEN

'BANKS ARE TO MAINTAIN TRUST

'THEY WANT RELATIONSHIP TECHNOLOGIES

IF/THEN PLAY

they repeat certain pages of the book, or that they print other pages in a single colour. Bismuth's input came late in the development of If/Then, forcing Mevis + van Deursen to rejig the layout completely; while most artists' interventions turn out to be little more than impotent gestures, Bismuth's contribution was an inescapable interference. By letting it happen, Mevis and van Deursen unequivocally demonstrated their allegiance to the rule of the system.

To bid for the identity scheme for Rotterdam 2001 – Rotterdam's stint as European Capital of Culture – Mevis + van Deursen produced a leaflet that introduced a set of simple, geometrical motifs on a 33mm grid (overleaf). The fresh colour scheme – pink, blue and green – shrugged off the weighty associations of the title 'Capital of Culture'.

The designers were commissioned for the project and worked with the notion that Rotterdam was not

If/Then was first conceived by Amsterdam-based designers Armand Mevis and Linda van Deursen as a journal; the publication's structure was intended to withstand repeated use and widely varying content. At the core of the design is a simple yet flexible grid system that holds together complex arrangements of text, image and graphic texture. On top of the grid is a very minimal identity scheme – a dotted line at the head and foot of each text page emphasizes folio headings. The

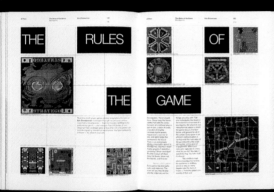

guiding idea behind the design was that each of the journal's spreads could be at the same time very different and unmistakably part of a single publication.

Leafing through If/Then, its most striking aspect is the lively, uneven pace. Each article's format is a response to its content, for example, an article on board games that illustrates the dual elements of gameplay – rules and randomness – is laid out on a square grid that simultaneously contains and is overrun by its subject. A further example is a timeline that turns the magazine on its side to offer a parallel exploration of the space race and the evolution of space-inspired play. Mevis + van Deursen's involvement in the journal went beyond the conventional definition of art direction and into the sphere of visual editing. Bringing a wide variety of imagery into the magazine, the designers created many of the powerful visual essays and striking juxtapositions that are evident across its pages. In their role as visual editors, Mevis and van Deursen also commissioned projects specifically for the journal. The most significant of these was an intervention by artist Pierre Bismuth, who set up a series of instructions for the designers, requiring, for example, that

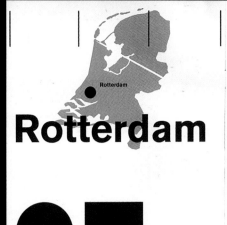

Rotterdam

Rotterdam

1/1
1/2
1/3
1/9
1/27

Combinations

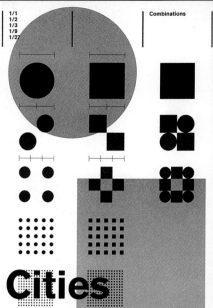

City

Cities

Rotterdam 2001
Culturele Hoofdstad
van Europa

Rotterdam 2001
Cultural Capital of
Europe

Rotterdam 2001
Capitale Culturelle
de l'Europe

Rotterdam 2001 Culturele Hoofdstad van Europa

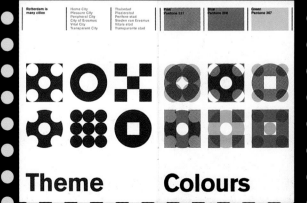

| Rotterdam is many cities | Home City
Pleasure City
Peripheral City
City of Erasmus
Vital City
Transparent City | Thuisstad
Pleizierstad
Perifere stad
Steden van Erasmus
Vitale stad
Transparante stad | Pink
Pantone 231 | Blue
Pantone 258 | Green
Pantone 367 |

Theme

Colours

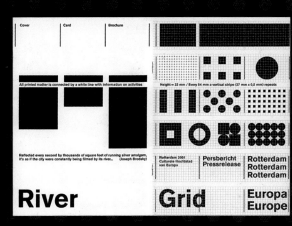

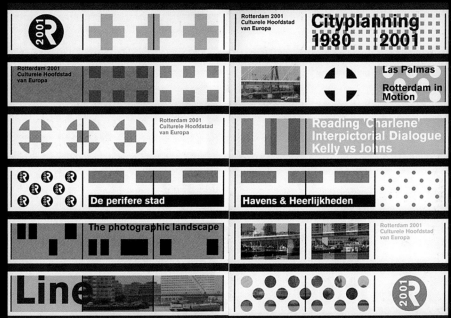

a single city but many cities (a theme derived from Italo Calvino's *Invisible Cities*). They sorted the activities and history of the city into a number of themes, and in response to these categories, Mevis and van Deursen presented the city with a set of basic designs – circles and squares that can be recombined to create endless alternatives. Faced with two sets – one of themes and one of design motifs – instinct urges us to partner a theme with a motif. In this case, however, it doesn't quite work.

Depending on how they are read, almost any symbol could be represented by any theme. By using a graphic language that suggests a straightforward and reductive relationship between form and content, Mevis and van Deursen have confounded expectation and delivered a teasing and elusive message. In effect, Rotterdam's identity scheme rides roughshod over the assumptions of graphic design.

Commissioned spreads for *Restart* [these pages–143], 2001

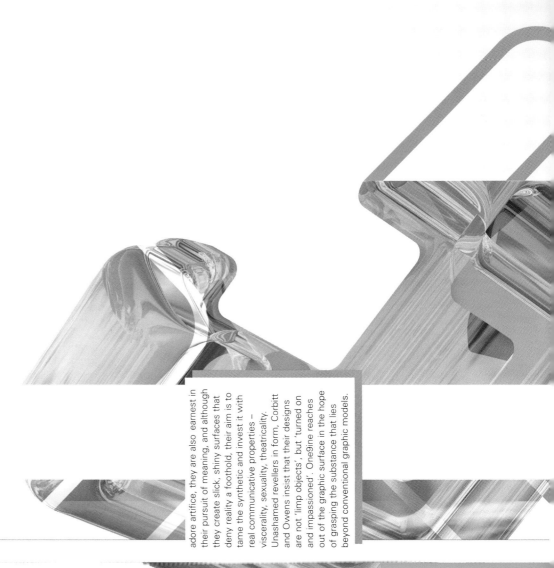

adore artifice, they are also earnest in their pursuit of meaning, and although they create slick, shiny surfaces that deny reality a foothold, their aim is to tame the synthetic and invest it with real communicative properties – viscerality, sexuality, theatricality. Unashamed revellers in form, Corbitt and Owens insist that their designs are not 'limp objects', but 'turned on and impassioned'. One9ine reaches out of the graphic surface in the hope of grasping the substance that lies beyond conventional graphic models.

The work of One9ine is fuelled by polarity: the persistent construction of dualities – flatness/depth, blue/orange, sharp/rounded, clamour/serenity, presence/absence – gives the studio's imagery a push-and-shove immediacy that is impossible to ignore. Let nothing be, spin it all around! What emerges is a restless system of communication, well-suited to what many believe to be a restless age.

Warren Corbitt and Matt Owens are Cranbrook graduates – Owens

under professors Michael and
Katherine McCoy and Corbitt
under the team P Scott Makela
and Laurie Haycock Makela – and
One9ine's design is informed by
the postmodern theory that has
suffused the school's approach
since the mid-1980s. Central to the
postmodern attitude adopted by
Cranbrook designers under the
tutelage of the McCoys was the
belief in the supremacy of the
subject. Later, under the Makelas,
Cranbrook designers remained

faithful to the reader, but
dramatically revised their view
of who that reader might be –
in place of a timid character
who might like to bring their
own experience to a text, they
envisaged a rapacious, media-
literate, image-hungry monster
who would gobble up not only
the text, but everything else
around it. Cranbrook graduates
have been aspiring to sate the
appetites of the reader ever
since. While graphic designers

emerging from the school
in the late-1980s offered
readers the chance to read
between the lines (a typical
device was to interweave
different passages of text),
the following generation of
Cranbrook designers present
readers with the opportunity
to gorge on gloss. Bridging
the two regimes, the
designers at One9ine
strive to do both.
    So while the designers

SITE LINES

A CONVERSATION FROM POINT A TO POINT B

[PATH?]

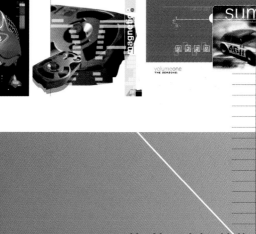

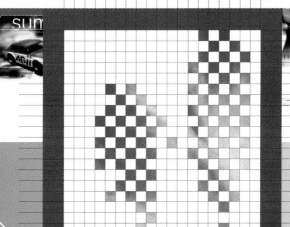

synthetic subjectivity

within...

the process of elocution and elucidation

unraveling

only to be reinvented anew

geometric objectivity

severed...

a methodology of representation

intertwined

an inverted evolution of the fragment

Wood scenes – slices of tree trunk printed with images of idealized natural environments – are available in gift shops throughout the US. Paul Sahre (New York) places them in the tradition of the home-made, remembering that his mother made them. The ones used here have either been bought or Sahre has made them himself.

Sahre does not distance himself from his source material in a manner that is characteristic of appropriation projects of this kind. His is not a

dislodge

dismiss

ditch

expel

forsake

leave

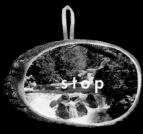

stop

vacate

wrest

camp take on the scenes, rather his work might be seen as an endorsement of the hopeless, romantic longing that they communicate. According to Sahre the 'intent was not to change the context of these objects by the addition of the words. The words are meant to point out paradoxes that are already inherent in the objects themselves, for example representing nature while destroying nature.'

The words that Sahre has

printed over the wood scenes relate to leaving, expulsion and loss. Superimposed on images of nature, the words speak sympathetically of the self-defeating nostalgia that informs a large part of mainstream environmental concern.

Band Identity for Gay Dad, 1999

By virtue of his matter-of-fact embodiment of two apparently contradictory characteristics, Gay Dad qualifies as the millennial everyman: an average citizen in a society that thrives on extremes. Peter Saville's Gay Dad is a pedestrian, a schematic arm-swinging stroller, but do not be deceived by his nonchalance. Gay Dad is a man on a mission: an everyday guy out to threaten those who still believe in the existence of everyday guys. In conjunction with

his child companions, Gay Dad taps
mercilessly into our conservative
reserves.

In the sleeve for Gay Dad's
debut album with London Records,
London-based Peter Saville included
a series of abstract, flat colour
compositions, made by rejigging
the parts of existing photographs
using software called Wave.
The images support the Gay Dad
programme by taking what we
already know, processing it and
offering it back to us in a way that

is somehow easy to swallow
and unnerving. The new world
is the old world taken apart
and reassembled in a novel
and disorienting fashion.

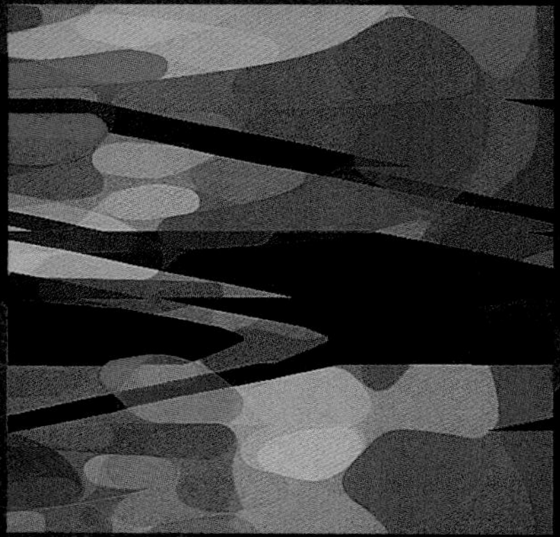

GUNS, DRUGS & NO MONEY

ORANGE BUSES

STARLINGS IN THE PLAZA

PICCADILLY PLAZA, GEORGE BEST, PIGEONS

Put forward by the citizens of Manchester, the phrases create a haze that obscures any singular city view – a fog redolent of many sulphurous, urban myths.

Peter Saville was commissioned to design a series of sleeve illustrations for the band Suede. He can be disarmingly frank about his sources, and casting around for a visual language that might resonate with Suede front man Brett Anderson, he came across a book of pictures by 1970s German surrealist Peter Wunderlicht. Anderson loved the

images (dodgy collages of airbrushed rainbows, body parts and the like) and they set about making their own versions.

Anderson chose the people and props – notably the mattress that dominates *Coming Up*, the first sleeve in the series – and Saville directed the photography and digital manipulation. The outcome is a collection of illustrations that create a disconcerting visual scheme: a lurid combination of the slick and the downbeat.

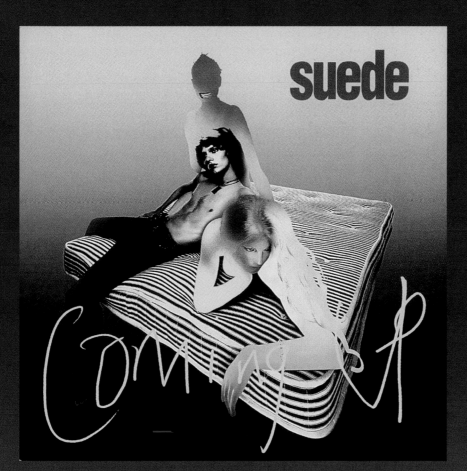

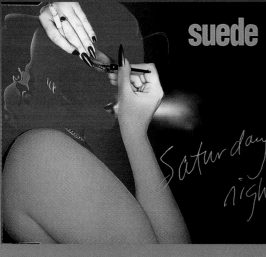

Cities are unfixed, multifaceted entities, and to ascribe an identity to a city is to risk producing an image that is either unsatisfactorily monodimensional or inappropriately bland; while your city isn't my city, everyone's city belongs

to no-one. Asked to design an identity for Manchester Records, Peter Saville skirted the dilemma by making a simple template – block capitals within an orange rectangle – that could contain any number of potentially conflicting urban snapshots: from the glamourously bleak 'Guns, Drugs & No Money' (surely the starting point of a film treatment?) to the factual 'Orange Buses'.

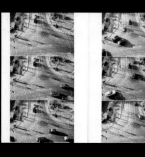

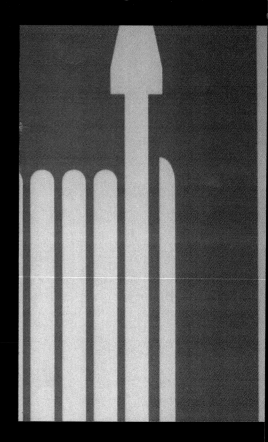

strike the chemical match abstractedly, blow out, strike, blow out, strike, speak a few words, blow out. He looked at the flame. He blew, he looked at the smoke. 'When will you be well?'
'Tomorrow. The next day maybe. First of the week.'
Beatty puffed his pipe. 'Every fireman, sooner or later, hits this. They only need understanding, to know how the wheels run. Need to know the history of our profession.
They don't feed it to rookies like they used to. Damn shame.'
Puff. 'Only fire chiefs remember it now.' Puff. I'll let you in on it.'
Mildred fidgeted. Beatty took a full minute to settle himself in and think back for what he wanted to say.
'When did it all start, you ask, this job of ours, how did it come about, where, when? Well, I'd say it really got started around about a thing called the Civil War. Even though our rule-book claims it was founded earlier. The fact is we didn't get along well until photography came into its own. Then – motion pictures in the early twentieth century. Radio. Television. Things began to have mass.'
Montag sat in bed, not moving.
'And because they had mass, they became simpler,' said Beatty. 'Once, books appealed to a few people, here, there, everywhere. They could afford to be different. The world was roomy. But then the world got full of eyes and elbows and mouths. Double, triple, quadruple population. Films and radios, magazines, books levelled down to a sort of paste pudding norm, do you follow me?'
'I think so.'
Beatty peered at the smoke pattern he had put out on the air. 'Picture it. Nineteenth-century man with his horses, dogs, carts, slow motion. Then, in the twentieth century, speed up your camera. Books cut shorter. Condensations. Digests. Tabloids. Everything boils down to the gag, the snap ending.'
'Snap ending.' Mildred nodded.
'Classics cut to fit fifteen-minute radio shows, then cut again to fill a two-minute book column, winding up at last as a ten- or twelve-line dictionary resume. I exaggerate, of course. The

Ray Bradbury Fahrenheit 451

The phrase 'paste pudding norm' was used by Ray Bradbury in the book *Fahrenheit 451* (Flamingo, 1993) to describe the cultural mulch of the mass media – the end product of more information, delivered more quickly to more people: 'Films and radios, magazines, books levelled down to a sort of paste pudding norm'.
Borrowing Bradbury's phrase, Philippin's book *the paste pudding norm* (kp books, 1999) appears to be no more than a collection of images.

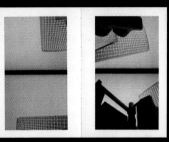

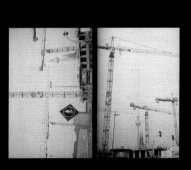

dictionaries were for reference. But many were those whose sole knowledge of Hamlet (you know the title certainly, Montag; it is probably only a faint rumour of a title to you, Mrs Montag) whose sole knowledge, as I say, of Hamlet was one-page digest in a book that claimed: now at least you can read all the classics; keep up with your neighbours. Do you see? Out of the nursery into the college and back to the nursery; there's your intellectual pattern for the past five centuries or more.'

Mildred arose and began to move around the room, picking things up and putting them down. Beatty ignored her and continued:

'Speed up the film, Montag, quick. Click? Pic? Look, Eye, Now, Flick, Here, There, Swift, Pace, Up, Down, In, Out, Why, How, Who, What, Where, Eh? Uh! Bang! Smack! Wallop, Bing, Bong, Boom! Digest-digests, digest-digest-digests. Politics? One column, two sentences, a headline! Then, in mid-air, all vanishes! Whirl man's mind around about so fast under the pumping hands of publishers, exploiters, broadcasters, that the centrifuge flings off all unnecessary, time-wasting thought!'

Mildred smoothed the bedclothes. Montag felt his heart jump and jump again as she patted his pillow. Right now she was pulling at his shoulder to try to get him to move so she could take the pillow out and fix it nicely and put it back. And perhaps cry out and stare or simply reach down her hand and say, 'What's this?' and hold up the hidden book with touching innocence.

'School is shortened, discipline relaxed, philosophies, histories, languages dropped, English and spelling gradually neglected, finally almost completely ignored. Life is immediate, the job counts, pleasure lies all about after work. Why learn anything save pressing buttons, pulling switches, fitting nuts and bolts?'

'Let me fix your pillow,' said Mildred.

'No!' whispered Montag.

'The zipper displaces the button and man lacks just that much

45

It is, however, intended to be a criticism of the surface values of the overblown picture books that have emerged from graphic designers over the last few years, and unlike those books *the paste pudding norm* yields another layer. Persistent readers will discover that tucked away inside its uncut pages is the entire text of Bradbury's *Fahrenheit 451*. Wilfully obscuring text with image, London-based Philippin creates a tension between the easily consumed

mass-media 'pudding' and the less digestible mass-media critique. To have one you must destroy the other.

In spite of its implied criticism of modern life, the top layer of *the paste pudding norm* is a well-paced picture essay compiled from a pleasingly idiosyncratic collection of photographs. Whatever his views on the ravages of the media, Philippin is unable to disguise his ability to savour the chewed-up, sloppy

mass of contemporary culture.

24 hours wall white, installation at the Royal College of Art, London, 1999

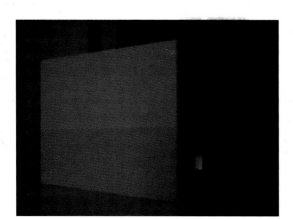

Standing in front of a source of natural light, the apparent shade of Philippin's piece *24 hours wall white* was in constant flux. The white wall, exhibited at the student show at the Royal College of Art in London, raises the question when is white white? Philosophically speaking you could argue always or never; the former if you prefer a use-based definition of colour, the latter if you are searching for the absolute essence of whiteness. There are other things going on here. In a gallery, whiteness is most often used as a device to banish the outside world. By propping his wall in front of a window, Frank Philippin turns the conventions of the white cube (as expressed by Brian Doherty in his seminal essay *Inside the White Cube*) inside out; white becomes a means of reflecting rather than refuting the environment beyond the confines of a gallery.

Philippin also designed the poster to advertise the show, putting a straight face (Helvetica) on a wilfully confrontational text.

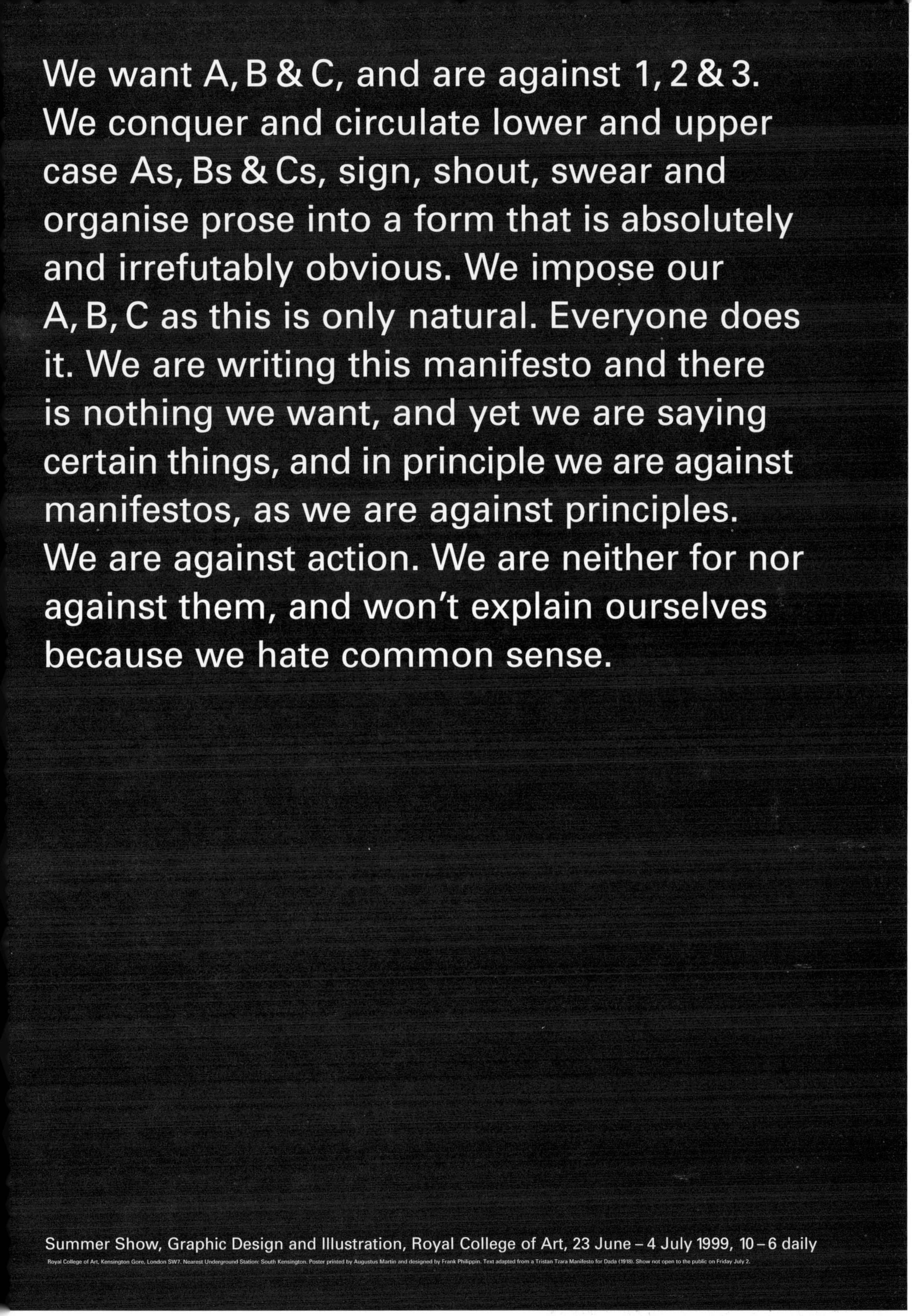

We want A, B & C, and are against 1, 2 & 3. We conquer and circulate lower and upper case As, Bs & Cs, sign, shout, swear and organise prose into a form that is absolutely and irrefutably obvious. We impose our A, B, C as this is only natural. Everyone does it. We are writing this manifesto and there is nothing we want, and yet we are saying certain things, and in principle we are against manifestos, as we are against principles. We are against action. We are neither for nor against them, and won't explain ourselves because we hate common sense.
Summer Show, Graphic Design and Illustration, Royal College of Art, 23 June – 4 July 1999, 10 – 6 daily
Royal College of Art, Kensington Gore, London SW7. Nearest Underground Station: South Kensington. Poster printed by Augustus Martin and designed by Frank Philippin. Text adapted from a Tristan Tzara Manifesto for Dada (1918). Show not open to the public on Friday July 2.

Frank Philippin

Poster advertising Royal College of Art exhibition, 1999

Catalogue for Schauspielhaus Zürich (photography: Isabel Truniger), 2000

JOSEF MEIER
Spezialist für Be- und Erleuchtung in der westlichen und östlichen Welt. In Zürich zeitweilig als Bühnentechniker.

150

MARCEL MEIER
Werbestrategisch versierter Generalist mit Faible für Verkauf, Inserate und Sponsoring. Geduldiger Texteintreiber in der Chaos-Kooperative Dramaturgie. Leiter Marketing & PR.

151

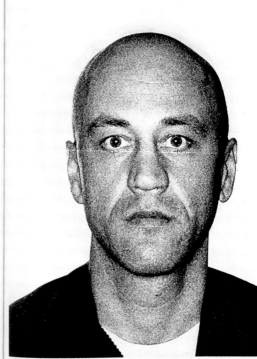

Cornel Windlin does not like irony. He is also suspicious of confrontational social critique in the style of Adbusters and the like. Both practices rely on a notion of normality, a belief in an everyday understanding that the ironist or provocateur can tease and twist. It is this assumption that Zürich-based Windlin rejects. Within his work, graphic meaning does not function according to a table of conventions, rather it is the product of makeshift clusters of associations. The

was distributed free of charge. The catalogue makes a straightforward anti-elitist point by displaying an equally sized image of each staff member and offering a short description of their role (theatre as part of everyday life, rather than outside it). In use, the catalogue has played as important a role within the theatre as beyond, becoming the primary means by which the staff can identify colleagues.

In *Autoland: Pictures from Switzerland* (overleaf), a book of

photographs of Swiss motorways taken by Nicholas Faure and edited by Cornel Windlin and Martin Heller, Windlin created an information system that, although visually reminiscent of the signage used on Switzerland's national roads, was entirely independent of existing graphic language. The style of Windlin's symbols implied straightforward and dispassionate communication, yet, scattered liberally throughout the book, they confound a direct reading. In fact,

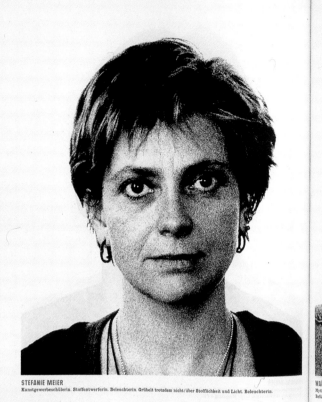

STEFANIE MEIER
Kunstgewerbeschülerin. Stoffentwerferin. Beleuchterin. Grübelt trotzdem nicht/über Stofflichkeit und Licht. Beleuchteria.

WALTER MILAN
Mythos in Zurigo South Side und Milano Centrale. Genannt «Key-man», «Bud Roses». Werkstättenleiter mit Allround- und All-around-Befähigung.

cascading through the air in a poster advertising an exhibition of Faure's photographs, the symbols become elements of chaos not markers of order. Faure aimed to record pictorially the Swiss motorway's condition, a system of roads that was established in the 1950s. In his editing and presentation of the photographs, Windlin stepped aside from Faure's documentary intent and drew the images together into a bleakly pretty visual poem.

Cornel Windlin has developed a sustained graphic language that is evident across his output, from motifs to symbols, from emblems to images. Although his work is dense with graphic clichés, widely used symbols and familiar decorative flourishes, it refuses to deliver what the audience expects. Windlin realigns ordinary graphic codes, allowing them to bear on the commonplace and at the same time to float free.

relationship between graphic form and graphic meaning built by Windlin – and his colleague Gilles Gavillet – is not dogmatic and is distinguished by its lightness of touch.

Most of Windlin's recent graphic design has been for the cultural sector, and although he works outside the commercial mainstream he is sensitive to the immediate promotional purpose of his output. Constructing a new communication policy for the Schauspielhaus Zürich (a major Swiss theatre), Windlin challenged the restrained good taste that governs advertising campaigns for cultural institutions. His proposal 'I Love Whatever' (overleaf) plastered the city with a series of slogans that proclaimed love (using the heart logo) for a range of feelings and objects. He described the project as 'meta-advertising' – the volume and clamour of advertising applied to oblique ends, a promotion of promotion itself. Aside from addressing advertising, the project is also about theatre; the city becomes a stage for language, phrases that in turn define the space and time of their occupation. As part of the same communication campaign, Windlin designed the Schauspielhaus Zürich season preview, a high-print-run catalogue (40,000) that

'I Love Whatever', communication concept for Schauspielhaus Zürich, 2000

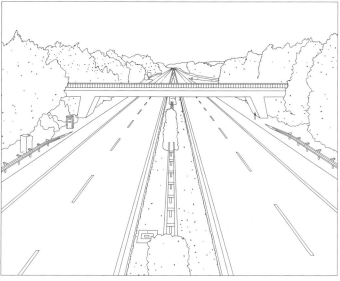

↗ NICOLAS FAURE: // AUTOLAND 유 유
↗ ↗ BILDER AUS DER SCHWEIZ
↗ PICTURES FROM SWITZERLAND

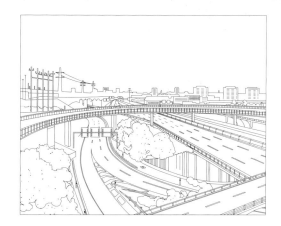

MUSEUM FÜR GESTALTUNG ZÜRICH

Cornel Windlin

Pages from *Autoland: Pictures from Switzerland*, book of photographs by Nicholas Faure, 1998 [left]
Poster advertising 'The Swiss Motorway', exhibition of Nicholas Faure's work, Museum für Gestaltung Zürich, 1999 [right]

Ganger Trilogy, audiovisual vinyl project, 1997

Much of the nostalgia attached
to vinyl recordings pertains to the
relationship between the record's
textured surface and the quality
of sound that it delivers. Invited
to collaborate on the creation of
a trilogy of vinyl records – three
remixes of a single track by Ganger
– Ian Wright and Bob Wilkinson
(London) chose to address the
relationship head-on.
    Attending the cutting of the
master disks of the *Ganger Trilogy*,
Wright and Wilkinson took the

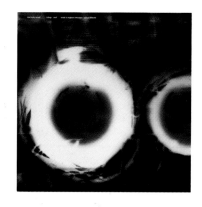

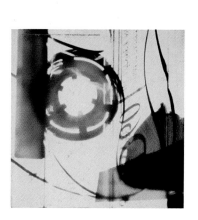

recordings fresh off the press and set to work on the B-side (a repeat of the A-side track) with scissors, metal brushes and knives. In each case, the texture created over the top of the record's grooves was a direct response to the attributes of the remix itself. An abstract mix prompted circular, damaged scratch patterns; a beat-based, minimal track inspired a series of regular grooves; and a hip-hop version suggested a worn-out, overplayed look. When the records

were produced at the pressing plant, the hand-made marks became the templates for the mass-produced objects. The gouged and scratched surfaces of the *Ganger Trilogy* lends the records an exaggerated presence. Just as book artists often adopt unwieldy or unusual formats to emphasize the materiality of the book, Wilkinson and Wright have purposefully overstated the physical properties of vinyl.

Many of the records were returned to the distributor because the B-side looks damaged and unplayable. Those brave enough to play them were rewarded with jumping, skipping, crunchy sounds, apparently enjoyed by the auditorially adventurous.

Michael Worthington

Commissioned work for *Restart* (this page–167), 2001

Seoul, Korea, 1999
Soo Jin Kim, photographer

The grid system is an aid, not a guarantee.

It seemed to us important to record the wide scope of a training system
which beyond a certain point is not experimental.

J.Müller-Brockmann
The Graphic Designer and His Design Problems,
1961, Verlag Arthur Niggli AG

St Ives, England, 1999
Michael John Worthington, graphic designer

Putting the personal picture in the impersonal frame

The modernist grid system, as a design aid, was undeniably an excellent system. It behaved logically and gave the indecisive designer concrete reasons for his actions, it made him feel as if he was doing the right thing. But like most strict systems it became predictable and ultimately familiar. It worked too well. It was too logical, too obedient. Or rather the designer believed in it totally, and his design development became plagued with premature obedience. Postmodernism rejected and broke the modernist grid, created the anti-grid, using formal signifiers of experimentation to produce a style-grid that eventually became as commodified and removed from its initial conceptual ideals as the modernist system had before it. It proved to be equally as confining. The grid system returned. Older and wiser. Initially as historical quotation but then, aware of its limitations, it was able to both surpass and redefine itself. The wheel of cool turned, and postmodernism became passé, while new modernism returned, rejuvenated. Reborn. Its agenda? To move beyond the arena of the training system and into the realm

of the experimental. This meant taking the impersonal visual system of modernism and investing it with a more personal system. Layers of systems, Russian dolls of meta systems. Because the modernist form was preordained to some extent, conceptual importance was placed on the system rather than formal detail, the system's ideas took precedent over the individual's ideas. In opposition to this, the current 'new modernism' calls for an individualistic, rather than an idealistic, system. Full modernism rather than empty modernism. The designer still creates the structure and lets the content run into it, yet the system has a life of its own. In the tradition of modernism, the structure grows out of the content: the material requires a certain space, and the rules the designer creates for that volume are systematically applied to the rest of the content. But when there is a disparity you see the gaps, the 'non-content' becomes visible, and the absences can be as interesting as the elements. The system used to be the idea. Now your system is the idea. Personal modernism rather than impersonal modernism.

When the formal attributes are so stripped down, each element (or non-element) gains significant importance. You focus closely on less items. You talk yourself out of anything that does not have conceptual importance. You must have a reason for everything. A conceptual rule for each formal element. The surface of modernism/minimalism becomes invested with designauthorialstructureconcepts. The system plays itself out. It creates narratives. The designer becomes a spectator of his own self-creating work. He plants the seed not knowing what will grow. the surprise can make the design experience fulfilling once more. The work takes over. turn it on itshead. use theimages to write the text not as secondaryelement to illustrate it. ironic/humorous, post modern humour without the formal-pastiche, simplesystem = singlenarrative, complexsystem = simultaneous/intertwining/ sub-andüber-narratives,don'tthink-aboutsemiotics,poststructuralism,embracingnoindividualvoice, embracethemundane,getundertheskinofthesystem,oncewe hadthevisiblegrid,nowwehavethevisibleconcept. worthington.

EVALUATE TO RE-EVALUATE

introduce slippage

seems to mean

AN INDIVIDUALISTIC,
RATHER THAN AN
IDEALISTIC, SYSTEM

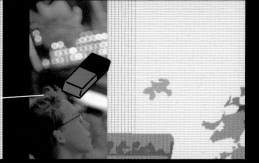

introduce personal narrative

Their system <u>was</u> the idea.
Now your system is the idea.

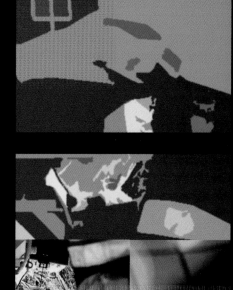

Simplification.
Isolation.
Looks good,
seems to mean ...

fella

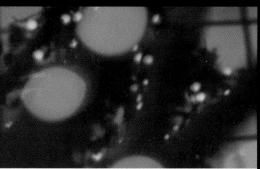

A training system
which beyond a
certain point is
not experimental.

müller-brockmann

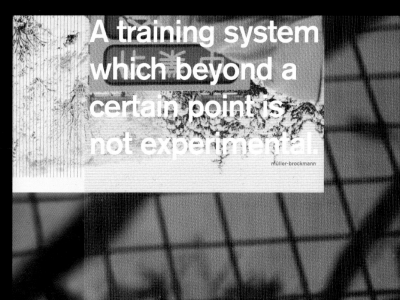

Q
When the design offers no distraction, are you directed
towards what's going on beneath the surface?

A1
The viewer searches for conceptual signifiers rather
than formal signifiers. Viewer becomes thinker.
Designer becomes thought provoker.

A2
Viewer gets bored. Turns page.

STYLISTIC INDIVIDUALITY

EXISTS WITHIN A SYSTEM

CONSISTING OF PREFORMED

COMPONENTS, ONLY WHEN

THE CONCEPT DRIVING

THE CONSTRUCTION IS

THOROUGHLY CONSIDERED

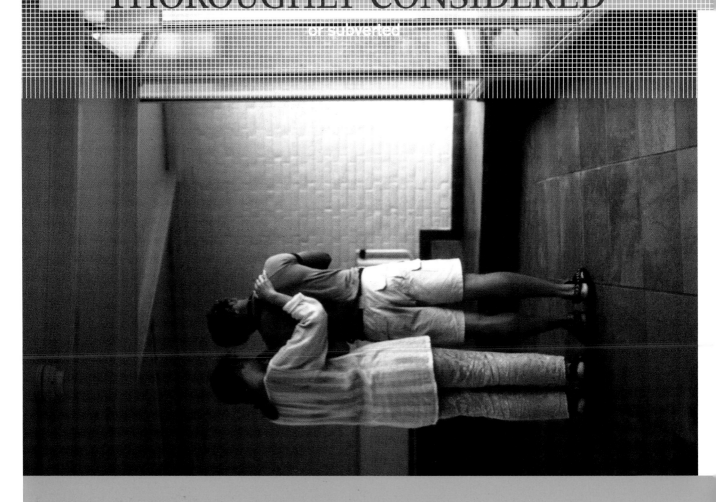

system for making this design:
1 record what you are thinking about right now
2 look at (ir)relevant historical references
3 gather content/concepts
4 manufacture the generic structure based on the
  restrictions implied by the volume of the content.
  start with generic sans type, generic image, solid
  cmyk, strict grid, rigid mathematics

MAKE
THE
SYSTEM
BREAK
THE
SYSTEM

worthington

5 disrupt the structure through the application of
  inflexible rules, specific to an instance, but applied
  to a series of elements:

  a.)
  b.)
  c.)
  d.)
  e.)

6 evaluate, introduce an idea/narrative and return to 5

CLAIM THE GENERIC AS YOUR OWN

CONSIDER THE TOO CONSIDERED

worthington

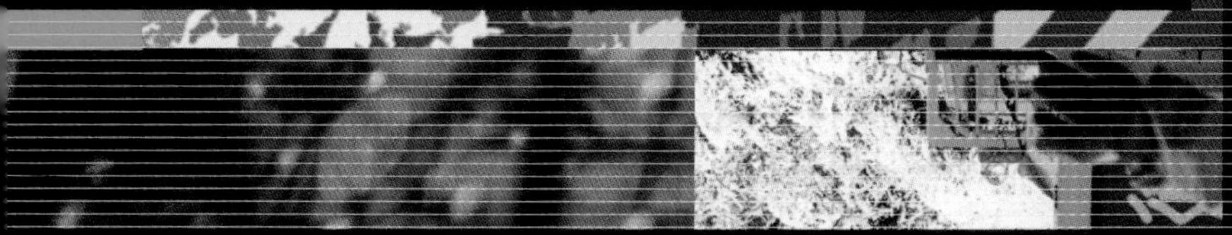

When the design offers no distraction
are you directed towards what's going
on beneath the surface?

CREATE A SLOGO
FOR YOUR
MINIFESTO

szyhalski

deck

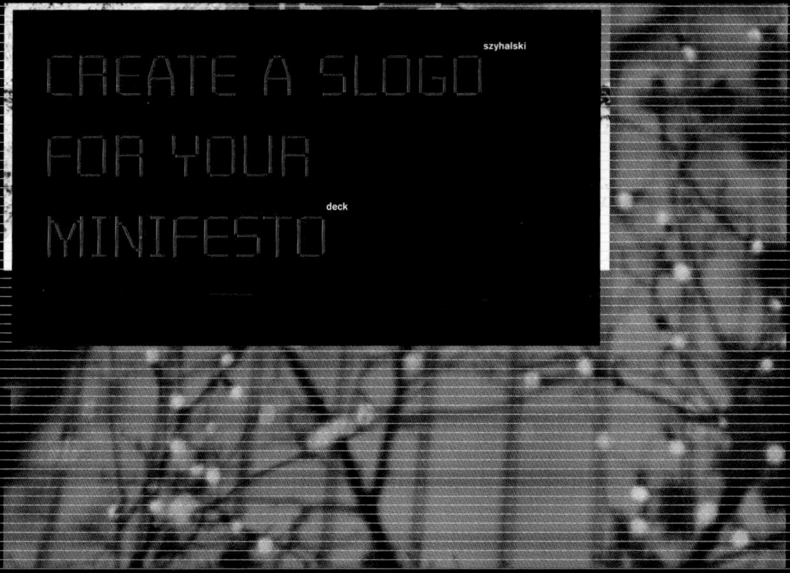

Amsterdam
Anaheim
Beijing
Brussels
Cornwall
Las Vegas
Seoul
Tokyo

photographs: Soo Jin Kim

IF YOU'RE SO CLEVER...

HOW COME DESIGN IS SO

DUMB?
kaliski/wild

commercial and art-based moving-image projects.
website: www.multiplex-tv.com
email: paul@multiplex-tv.com

JAKE TILSON (86–91)

Atlas, websites, 24 hours, collages, architecture, magazines, sculpture, 'The Cooker', books, vernacular, audio works, faxes, cities, Cipher, inkjet prints, 'The Terminator Line', video works, food, photographs, Xeroxes, found, urban, distributed art, Vulture Reality, everyday, dioramas, travel, Peckham. We are happy to serve you.
website: www.thecooker.com
website: www.araaatlas.com
email: jake@thecooker.com

2x4 (96–101)

Founded in 1994 by Michael Rock, Susan Sellers and

Georgianna Stout, 2x4 is a New York-based team of creative directors, writers and designers working with such diverse clients as The New York Times and the Office for Metropolitan Architecture (OMA). Michael Rock is associate professor of design at Yale University's School of Art in New Haven and a fellow at the Jan van Eyck Academy in Maastricht, the Netherlands. He is a contributing editor to I.D. in New York and his writing has also appeared in a variety of international publications. Susan Sellers is a writer and designer, as well as a lecturer at Yale University School of Art. Her articles have appeared in a number of journals, including Eye, Design Issues and Visible Language. Sellers concentrated on early-twentieth-century material culture for her MA in American Studies at Yale University. Georgianna Stout was previously an associate of New York's Bethany Johns Design where her clients included

British Design'. His writing has been published in Eye magazine and in the Tokyo-based design journal IDEA. He cycles with Critical Mass in New York, which meets in Union Square at 7pm on the last Friday of every month.
website: otherschools.com
email: paul.elliman@yale.edu

MILES MURRAY SORRELL [FUEL] (70–71)

Since 1991, London-based designers Peter Miles, Damon Murray and Stephen Sorrell have worked together as a graphic-design group. They produced seven issues of Fuel magazine before they published their first book rave Fuel in 1996. Their second book Fuel 3000 (London: Laurence King Publishing) came out in 2000.
website: www.fuel-design.com
email: fuel@fuel-design.com

GRAPHIC THOUGHT FACILITY (72–75)

Andy Stevens and Paul Neale met while studying for their MAs at London's Royal College of Art between 1988 and 1990. After graduation they founded GTF and have been working together ever since, joined in 1997 by Steffi Orazi and in 1998 by Huw Morgan. Graphic Thought Facility is concerned with process, juxtaposition and observational reference. Alongside a wide range of small-scale cultural projects, they have produced a larger body of ongoing work for furniture retailer Habitat.
email: info@graphicthoughtfacility.com

MÜLLER + HESS (76–81)

Zürich-based design group Müller + Hess combines self-published work (the magazine Grenzwert) with design for cultural institutions, such as the Basel Art Fair. Beat Müller, Wendlin Hess, Michael Birchmeier and Ludovic Balland, all members of

40 Under 30 in 2000. In 2001, Barth formed the design collective stiletto in New York along with Julie Hirschfeld and Joan Raspo. Stiletto works with a variety of media: film, animation, motion graphics, print and the Web.
website: www.stilettonyc.com
email: stefanie@stilettonyc.com

TOMATO INTERACTIVE (50–53)

The studio was formed in the early summer of 1999 by Joel Baumann, Antony Rogers and Tom Roope, all three were former members of the Anti-rom team and each had a strong creative relationship with design group Tomato. London-based Tomato Interactive has worked with Sony on an international on-line identity, with Levi's ICD+ (a collaboration between the Levi's brand and Philips on a new range of clothing) on CD-ROMs and a website and with Mitsubishi Motors in

Japan on a website. The designers have also collaborated with Ron Arad and the Busaba Eathai Restaurant in London. Tomato Interactive was awarded a silver medal at D&AD (Design and Art Direction) 2000 and the CD tomato three' won the studio a BIMA (British Interactive Multimedia Association) Award in 2000.
website: www.tomato.co.uk
email: mail@tomato.co.uk

BUMP (58–61)

Mike Watson and Jon Morgan's London-based graphic-design unit is called Bump. Watson and Morgan play off the combination of the raw, wicked and banal of the culture that surrounds them. Bump points out the details, isolating and repositioning them with a sharp sense of irony that simultaneously celebrates and disturbs. Watson and Morgan have

graphic and interior design. Andreas Lauhoff holds an MA (1998) in graphic design from Central Saint Martins College of Art and Design in London.
website: www.3deluxe.de
email: a.lauhoff@3deluxe.de

JOHN MAEDA (28–33)

Sony career development professor of media arts and sciences and associate professor of design and computation at the Massachusetts Institute of Technology Media Laboratory in Cambridge, Massachusetts, John Maeda also directs the Aesthetics and Computation Group. He received undergraduate and graduate degrees in computer science from M.I.T. after which he went to Japan to study art and design at the University of Tsukuba Institute of Art and Design. His goal is to develop 'humanist technologists' – people who can make

creative decisions that simultaneously result in culturally relevant and technologically innovative artefacts. Maeda is the recipient of the DaimlerChrysler Award for Innovation in Design.
website: www.maedastudio.com
email: maeda@media.mit.edu

SARA MACONKEY (34–35)

Since graduating from London's Royal College of Art in 1999, Sara Maconkey has worked as a freelance designer in London and Venice. She worked at Greenpeace for several months and continues to advise the organization on its digital strategy. Now living in Edinburgh Maconkey designs for the Web at Realise.
email: sara@realise.com

NORM (36–43)

JOSHUA BERGER/PLAZM (14–17)

Founded in 1991 by a group of artists in Portland, Oregon, Plazm Media publishes an eclectic design magazine with worldwide distribution. The company also operates an innovative type foundry and conducts business as a design firm, with such clients as Lucasfilm, MTV and Nike. Plazm has won numerous awards, including the 100 Show award of merit in 1998, and the group's work has been featured in many international publications. Issues 1–21 of Plazm Magazine are part of the San Francisco Museum of Modern Art's permanent collection.
website: www.plazm.com
email: josh@plazm.com

PAUL FARRINGTON/TONNE (18–23)

London-based designer Paul Farrington, also known

The Andy Warhol Museum in Pittsburgh and the Dia Center for the Arts (formerly Dia Art Foundation) in New York. Alongside her work with 2x4, Stout collaborates with sculptor David Weeks to produce print and furniture design.
website: www.twoxfour.net
email: michael@twoxfour.net

ALEXANDER BOXILL (102–05)
(Jayne Alexander and Violetta Boxill)
Past: long hours; good fun
Present: long hours; good fun; money
Future: less hours; more fun; more money
website: www.alexanderboxill.com
email: info@alexanderboxill.com

PETER ANDERSON (106–09)
At Central Saint Martin's College of Art and Design,

Müller + Hess, were trained in the Swiss school of typography and their graphic work is characterized by the sophisticated subversion of this typographic tradition.
website: www.muellerhess.ch
email: info@muellerhess.ch

PAUL PLOWMAN (82–85)
Between 1987 and 1990, Paul Plowman studied graphic design at Leeds Metropolitan University (UK). He then spent from 1991 to 1993 working on an his MA in graphics at the Royal College of Art. In partnership with Lol Sargent, Plowman set up a graphics company called Simple Productions that creates TV titles and graphics and video-installation exhibition design. On leaving Simple in 1999 Plowman formed the Multiplex TV project in London with Anthony Burrill. They work on a broad range of

designed publications, exhibitions, advertising and identities, and their work has been featured in such exhibitions as 'Stealing Beauty' (ICA, April 1999) and 'Designs On the Village Fete' (Victoria and Albert Museum, July 2000).
website: www.bumptown.co.uk
email: bump@btconnect.com

ANTHONY BURRILL (62–65)
After graduating from the Royal College of Art in 1991, Anthony Burrill established Bless the Artist, his own London-based design studio. He has published many short books, produced on corner-shop photocopiers (titles include Sweetshop and Hi-Lo-Fi). At the same time, he has worked in advertising, television and design, most notably creating award-winning advertising for the Hans Brinker Budget Hotel in Amsterdam with the

advertising agency KesselsKramer. In 1996 he was nominated for a Creative Future in Internet design by Creative Review magazine; in 1997 Burrill and Kip Parker set up Friendchip, an Internet design project, and the pair have worked on a range of projects, such as the Kraftwerk website.
website: www.friendchip.com
email: anthony@friendchip.com

PAUL ELLIMAN (66–69)
Assistant professor at Yale School of Art in New Haven and project tutor at the Jan van Eyck Academy in Maastricht, the Netherlands, Paul Elliman has exhibited at Tate Modern in London and examples of his work appear in the British Arts Council's travelling collection 'Lost and Found: Critical Voices in New

Dimitri Bruni and Manuel Krebs graduated from Switzerland's Biel School of Design in 1996. They worked for design studios in Zürich and Geneva before founding Norm on 1 January 1999. The Zürich studio produces its own publications and font designs alongside more general graphic design. In 2000 Bruni and Krebs published Introduction.

website: www.norm.to
email: n@norm.to

RALPH STEINBRÜCHEL (44–47)
Between 1997 and 1998, Ralph Steinbrüchel studied for an MA in communication design at Central Saint Martins College of Art and Design in London. He has since been working as a freelance designer in Zürich, Switzerland and also makes electronic music. Steinbrüchel is in the process of

setting up a new label, synchron, which will focus on the release of experimental electronic music and on projects that combine music with graphics and animation.
website: www.synchron.ch
email: steinbrüchel@synchron.ch

STEFANIE BARTH (48–49)
A graduate of the Hochschule für Gestaltung in Offenbach Am Main, Germany, Stefanie Barth has worked as a graphic designer in Frankfurt since 1995. She concentrates on projects for print and screen, including vinyl covers, corporate designs, film titles, Web pages and on-air designs for VH1 in New York. She compiled and designed Pause :59 Minutes of Motion Graphics with Julie Hirschfeld, with whom she featured in I.D.'s

as Tonne, has made visible the work of such musicians as Scanner, Pole and SpringHeel Jack by linking sound with an image that varies between the elegant simplicity of lines and superimposed layers. Developing and producing controlled systems for sound and image interaction. Tonne has performed live at Sónar – International Festival of Advanced Music and Multimedia Art (Barcelona, Spain), Montréal International Festival of New Cinema and New Media (Canada), Expanded Cinema (Milan, Italy), Lovebytes Digital Arts Festival (Sheffield, UK) and Steim – Studio for Electro-Instrumental Music (Amsterdam, the Netherlands). Tonne was named the up-and-coming graphic designer of 1999 at Creative Review's annual event Creative Futures. Tonne has also been commissioned by music label Meta to release recordings of his sound toys.

website: www.tonne.org.uk
email: studio@tonne.org.uk

HENRIK KUBEL + SCOTT WILLIAMS (24–25)
Henrik Kubel and Scott Williams formed London-based design studio A2-GRAPHICS/SW/HK while studying for an MA at the Royal College of Art. Williams graduated with first-class honours in graphic design from the University of Salford (UK) in 1998 and Kubel left Denmark's Design School in Copenhagen with a BA in 1997. As a multidisciplinary design collaborative, A2-GRAPHICS/SW/HK works on print, new media and conceptual projects. Currently the studio is researching the representation and classification of colour and preparing for the launch of an on-line type shop. Kubel and Williams have participated in

several international exhibitions, including 'Lost and Found' in Stockholm (Sweden, 2001), and have received several student awards from The Art Directors Club, New York, and D&AD (Design and Art Direction), London.
website: www.a2-graphics.co.uk
email: info@a2-graphics.co.uk

ANDREAS LAUHOFF (26–27)
After graduating in graphic design from FH Wiesbaden in 1992, Andreas Lauhoff founded the design group 3deluxe with Stephan Lauhoff and Nick Schweiger (the group was completed in 1997 by the addition of a fourth member, Dieter Brell). Since then, the designers have been working on a fluid interface between

King has begun to concentrate on solo work and is represented by Magnani Gallery, London.
email: scottking@magnani.co.uk

MITSUO KATSUI (122–25)
Tokyo-based designer Mitsuo Katsui was among the first graphic designers to use computers in the graphic process. From the late 1960s, he has realized ambitious projects and is a leading member of the Japan Computer Graphics Association, which helps to organize the NICOGRAPH exhibition and conference for computer graphics. He has designed posters for conferences, exhibitions and significant international events, such as the Hiroshima appeal. Katsui has exhibited his work in the US, The Czech Republic, Poland and China.
email: kdo-001@fd.catv.ne.jp

M/M (126–29)
The Paris-based design group was founded in 1992 by Michael Amzalag and Mathias Augustyniak. Their early work was largely for the music industry, but they have since moved into other fields of graphic design. M/M has designed many catalogues and books for art institutions, working closely with such artists as Philippe Parreno, Inez van Lamsweerde, Pierre Huyghe, Dominique Gonzalez-Foerster. The studio is also very involved in fashion, producing catalogues and campaigns for, among others, Yohji Yamamoto, Balenciaga, Louis Vuitton, Martine Sitbon and Jil Sander. Maintaining an interest in music, M/M has created images for Björk that are to become part of a book project. Amzalag and Augustyniak believe that it is strategically important to become involved in projects of very different scales.

Peter Boyd Joines Anderson followed a BA in graphic design with a postgraduate degree in fine art printmaking and photomedia. Since graduating in 1994, he has designed artists' books that have been collected by numerous institutions, including the Victoria and Albert Museum. He has contributed to many international exhibitions and his work has been published in such magazines as Eye and The Independent Magazine. Joining design group Interfield in 1997, he has worked for clients like Harvey Nichols, Hilton Worldwide and Channel Four.
website: www.interfield-design.com
email: peter@interfield.freeserve.co.uk

IRMA BOOM (110–11)
Since founding her own studio in Amsterdam in 1991, Irma Boom has won many awards for her design of books, catalogues, annual reports and

and Printed Letters: The Natural History of Typography. Miller edits and designs 2wice magazine, which was awarded magazine of the year from The Society of Publication Designers. Miller is a partner at the New York office of international design consultancy Pentagram.
email: miller@pentagram.com/eilupton@x.netcom.com

MEVIS + VAN DEURSEN (134–37)
Armand Mevis and Linda van Deursen studied at the Gerrit Rietveld Academy in Amsterdam, following which they have made catalogues for the Stedelijk Museum of Modern Art in Amsterdam, posters for the Muziektheater in Amsterdam and stamps for the Dutch post office (KPN). Their work has been published in Eye, Emigre, Typography Now, The Graphic Edge (Poynor, Rick, Booth-Clibborn Editions, 2000) and I.D. Forty. Mevis and van Deursen's work has been

exhibited internationally and they have conducted workshops at educational institutions in Europe and the US.
website: www.ifthen.org
email: mevd@xs4all.nl

ONE9INE (138–43)
Formed in the summer of 1999 by Warren Corbitt and Matt Owens, both graduates of the Cranbrook Academy's department of art, the New York studio One9ine specializes in visual communication for print, broadcasting and interactive media. Seeking to play in the space where divergent media begin to commingle, One9ine exploits the very space that traditional media categorization aims to disqualify. Clients include Bartle Bogle Hegarty, Museum of Modern Art and the United Nations. Prior to forming One9ine, Corbitt codesigned WhereIsHere

designers Jil Sander and Yohji Yamamoto and with art institutions, such as London's Whitechapel Art Gallery and Paris's Centre Georges Pompidou. Saville now concentrates on his own creative projects (for example, SHOWstudio, a multi-media workshop conceived with Nick Knight) and on consulting for corporate clients.
website: www.showstudio.com

FRANK PHILIPPIN (150–53)
After working as a designer in Stuttgart and Hamburg between 1990 and 1994, Frank Philippin moved to London where he gained a BA in graphic design from Camberwell College of Arts and an MA from the Royal College of Art. Leaving the RCA in 1999, he established his London-based studio Brighten The Corners, where he works on book projects, such as Staircases by Eva Jiricna (published in 2001), and contributes to exhibitions.
website: www.brightenthecorners.com

email: brightenthecorners@lineone.net

CORNEL WINDLIN (154–57)
Q. Major Clients?
A. (Selection): Procter & Gamble, Polaroid, Union Bank of Switzerland (UBS), Sony, The Nelson Mandela Trust Inc., Nestlé, Novartis, Universal, Time Life Inc., Sumitomo, American Steel Corporatico, Lockheed, DaimlerChrysler, Tate Japan, The Singapore Gucci Tate, The Beijing Armani Guggenheim Foundation, The GuggenMoma (Europe) Corporation.
Q. Significant projects?
A. United Nations Peace Corps logo redesign.
Q. Publications/awards?
A. Awards are slimy.
Q. The single most important thing you would like to communicate about yourself to the reader?
A. 1. Design seemed like a good idea at the time.

Arts and making portraits.
website: www.mriamwright.co.uk
email: sans@ditcon.co.uk

MICHAEL WORTHINGTON (160–67)
Codirector of the graphic design programme at California Institute of the Arts, Michael Worthington also runs the small, Los Angeles–based Worthington Design. His work includes design writing, editorial projects and graphic design and typography for print and screen.
website: design.calarts.edu
email: marfish@earthlink.net

CHRISTIAN KÜSTERS
Graduating from the London College of Printing, Christian Küsters went on to Yale University, where he was awarded an MFA in graphic design in 1995. He has since established CHK Design, his own London-based company,

and launched Acme Fonts, a digital type foundry. Küsters teaches at Camberwell College of Arts and is art director of Architectural Design magazine. He has written for such magazines as Eye, Baseline and Graphics International.
website: www.acmefonts.net
email: christian@chkdesign.demon.co.uk

EMILY KING
Holding an MA in design history from London's Royal College of Art, Emily King also has a PhD from Kingston University that addresses the design of typefaces in the first decade after the introduction of desk-top-publishing technology. She is design editor of Frieze magazine and a regular contributor to design publications, including Eye. King taught history of design at the RCA for five years.
email: emily@frieze.co.uk

postage stamps. Her work has been exhibited internationally and in 1998 she held a solo exhibition at the Stroom Centre for Visual Arts, The Hague. She has lectured and conducted workshops at educational institutions across Europe and the United States: between 1998 and 2000 she was a tutor at the Jan van Eyck Academy in Maastricht, the Netherlands, and since 1992 she has been a lecturer at Yale University, New Haven.

email: irmaboom@xs4all.nl

DARREN HUGHES (112-13)
London-based designer Darren Hughes holds a BA in graphic design from Camberwell School of Arts and an MA from the Royal College of Art. He is particularly interested in the use of graphic design for political and environmental ends.

email: mrdarrenhughes@ hotmail.com

ANGUS HYLAND (114-15)
Angus Hyland studied at the London College of Printing and went on to the Royal College of Art, graduating in 1988. He then ran his own London-based studio and, in 1998, became a principal at Pentagram Design. His projects include corporate identity, book publishing, fashion campaigns, commercials, record sleeves and information and exhibition design. Hyland has worked with a wide range of clients, such as the Crafts Council, Shakespeare's Globe Theatre, BMP DDB, BBC, Virgin Classics and Getty Images. Exhibited and published internationally, he is author of *Pen and Mouse* (London: Laurence King Publishing, 2001), a book on contemporary illustration.

Hyland has taught at the London College of Printing and The Domus Academy in Milan.

email: hyland@pentagram.co.uk

SCOTT KING (116-21)
Between 1993 and 1996, Scott King was art director of *i.D*, following which he founded *Crash* with writer and historian Matthew Worley. *Crash* initially took the form of an 'agit-pop' (sic) magazine, but the project has been expanded into many forms to include billboards, advertisements, magazine commissions and 'solo' and group shows in the UK and Europe. In December 1999 King and Worley curated 'Crash', a group show at London's Institute of Contemporary Arts.

website: www.mmparis.com
email: anyone@mmparis.com

BRUCE MAU (130-31)
Establishing his reputation with the design of *Zone 1/2* in 1986, Toronto-based Bruce Mau has collaborated with a range of cultural organizations and contemporary artists and architects, including the Getty Research Institute, Tate Gallery, Art Gallery of Ontario, The Netherlands Architecture Institute, Frank O. Gehry, Claes Oldenburg, Michael Snow and Douglas Gordon. In 1996, Mau coauthored the critically acclaimed *S,M,L,XL* (Benedikt Taschen Verlag, 1997) with architect Rem Koolhaas. His book, *Life Style*, was published by Phaidon Press in 2000.
website: www.brucemaudesign.com
email: studio@brucemaudesign.com

ELLEN LUPTON AND J. ABBOTT MILLER (132-33)
Curator of comtemporary design at the Cooper-Hewitt, National Design Museum (Smithsonian Institution) in New York, Ellen Lupton also co-chairs the graphic-design programme at Maryland Institute, College of Art in Baltimore with J. Abbott Miller. She has organized numerous exhibitions, including 'Mechanical Brides: Women and Machines from Home to Office' (1993) and 'National Design Triennial: Design Culture Now' (2000).
Designer, writer, curator and educator, J. Abbott Miller concerns himself with the cultural role of design. His exhibitions and publications include *The Process of Elimination: The Bathroom, the Kitchen and the Aesthetics of Waste* (with Ellen Lupton)

(London: Laurence King Publishing, 1998) with P. Scott Makela and Laurie Haycock-Makela and worked on numerous other publication designs. Owens launched volumeone, a design studio dedicated to pushing the limits of available on-line design technologies.
website: www.one9ine.com
email: warren@one9ine.com

PAUL SAHRE (144-45)
Hand-printing posters for such non-profit institutions as the Fells Point Corner Theatre in Baltimore and the Soho Repertory Theatre in New York, Paul Sahre also designs book covers for the publishing houses Beacon Press, Alfred A. Knopf, Vintage Books, Little, Brown and Company and Verso. His work ranges from traditional print media to new media design. Sahre recently moved from

his one-man design office to become associate partner in Doyle Partners, New York. He received a BFA and an MFA in graphic design from Kent State University in Ohio and now teaches graphic design and typography at Parsons School of Design and at the Cooper Union School of Art, both in New York.
email: officeofps@earthlink.net

PETER SAVILLE (146-49)
Now London-based, Peter Saville made his name twenty years ago as art director and co-founder of Factory Records in Manchester, where he created iconic graphics for such bands as Joy Division and New Order. Alongside his sustained relationship with the music industry (clients include Suede and Pulp) he also works extensively with fashion

2. Things first!
3. Why?
website: www.ilovepeanutbutter.org
email: cornelwindlin@lineto.com

IAN WRIGHT AND BOB WILKINSON (158-59)
Ian Wright has been a freelance illustrator since 1978. 'He's still doing it', says Bob Wilkinson. The relationship is less Charles and Ray and more Han and Chewy. Meeting at Neville Brody's research studios, Wright and Wilkinson found themselves united by a passion for music and have since collaborated on a variety projects. Wilkinson works with Lucienne Roberts at sans-baum, where they have a broad range of clients from arts-related to charity-based institutions. He is a signatory of the *First Things First* manifesto. Wright balances his working life by teaching at Camberwell College of

The type in *Restart* is set in Univers by Christian Küsters according to a grid system derived from Adrian Frutiger's 1957 diagrammatic display of the typeface. Frutiger arranged all twenty-one versions of his font family in a grid, the position of each decided by its relative weight and style, making clear the underlying principle of Univers: that each version of the font can be understood in correspondence with the others. The principle is also expressed in the pioneering system of nomenclature that Frutiger applied to the Univers typeface, every variant being given a numeric subtitle that quantitatively describes its position vis-à-vis its fellows. In Küsters's arrangement, the text flows

- Kinross, Robin. *Modern Typography: An Essay in Critical History* (London: Hyphen Press, 1992).
- Lupton, Ellen & J. Abbott Miller. *Design, Writing, Research: Writing on Graphic Design* (London: Phaidon Press, 1999).
- Poynor, Rick. Booth-Clibborn, Edward, ed. *Typography Now: The Next Wave* (London: Booth-Clibborn Editions, 1994).
- Poynor, Rick. *Design Without Boundaries: Visual Communication in Transition* (London: Booth-Clibborn Editions, 1998).
- Rand, Paul. *Thoughts on Design* (New York: Wittenborn & Co., 1947. Rev. ed. London: Studio Vista, New York: Van Nostrand Reinhold Co., 1970).
- Tschichold, Jan. Trans. by Ruari McLean. *The New Typography* (Berkeley, CA: University of California Press, 1995).
- Wozencroft, Jon. *The Graphic Language of Neville Brody* (London: Thames & Hudson, 1988).

CREDITS

p. 13. Extension to the Jewish Museum Daniel Libeskind, photograph by Hélène Binet.

pp. 56–57. [clockwise, from bottom left] *Christine* by Julian Opie at Lisson Gallery; Walker typeface designed for The Walker Arts Center by Matthew Carter, 1995; 'Personal Panel' by Andrea Zittel at Sadie

Sring/Summer 1999 catalogues: photography Inez van Lamsweerde & Vinoodh Matadin; Fall/Winter 2000/2001 catalogue: photography Craig McDean.

p. 129. project coordinated by Fabrice Hergott and catalogue published by Editions du Centre Pompidou, Paris.

Bruce Mau
p. 131. Book to accompany the 'Douglas Gordon • Black Spot' exhibition printed by Tate Gallery Publishing.

Ellen Lupton and J. Abbott Miller
p. 133. Brick books produced by Kiosk.

Mevis + van Deursen

pp. 134–35. *If/Then* edited by Jan Abrams and published by Netherlands Design Institute.

Peter Saville
pp. 146–47. Band identity for Gay Dad. Graphic art: Peter Saville with Howard Wakefield and Paul Hetherington; logo concept: Paul Barnes.
p. 148. Identity for Manchester Records. Graphic art: Peter Saville and Howard Wakefield.
p. 149. Record sleeve illustrations for Suede. Graphic art: Peter Saville, Nick Knight and Howard Wakefield.

Frank Philippin

ACKNOWLEDGMENTS

Many thanks for their advice: Nick Bell, Ferdy Carabott, Richard Green, David Israel, Alice Twemlow and Peter B. Willberg.
    Special thanks to Liz Farelly for her support in the early stages of this project and to Lucas Dietrich and Catherine Hall at Thames & Hudson for their advice throughout.

Warmest thanks to all contributors!

Book concept: Christian Küsters
Edited by Christian Küsters + Emily King
All texts: Emily King
Design: Christian Küsters
Design assistant: Owen Peyton Jones

Cover and divider images by Sølve Sundsbø.
3D manipulation by Antony Crossfield @ Metro Imaging Ltd.

Thank you to Mario @ Metro Imaging Ltd. 020 7543 4040

This version of Univers was kindly donated by CPS

First published in the United Kingdom in 2001 by Thames & Hudson Ltd, 181A High Holborn, London WC1V 7QX

© 2001 Christian Küsters and Emily King

All Rights Reserved. No part of this publication may be reproduced or transmitted in any form or by any means, electronic or mechanical, including photocopy, recording or any other information storage and retrieval system, without prior permission in writing from the publisher.

British Library Cataloguing-in-Publication Data
A catalogue record for this book is available from the British Library

ISBN 0-500-28297-8

Printed and bound in Hong Kong by C & C Offset

freely and typographic anomalies stand as evidence of the system at work.

A second grid system operates independently from the first. The illustration grid is constructed from the dimensions of the 1925 DIN (Deutsche Industrie Norm) paper system, meaning that all illustrations are deliberately sized to fall between A3 and A8. The placement of the images on the page is not random: a third grid system is based on the length and width measurements of these paper sizes. As a result the size of each image in the book (where possible) bears a systematic relationship to the grid on that particular page.

The title of the book is set in every version of Univers that is used across its pages, overlaid, one on top of the other. The titles that appear throughout the book are rendered in a selective collision of Univers fonts, the composition of each being determined by the type used in the boxes on the same horizontal line.

BIBLIOGRAPHY

- Bierut, Michael, William Drenttel, Steven Heller, and D. K. Holland, eds. *Looking Closer: Critical Writings on Graphic Design* (New York: Allworth Press, 1996).
- Bierut, Michael, William Drenttel, Steven Heller, and D. K. Holland, eds. *Looking Closer 2: Critical Writings on Graphic Design* (New York: Allworth Press, 1997).
- Broos, Kees and Paul Hefting. *Dutch Graphic Design: A Century* (London: Phaidon Press, 1998).
- Friedman, Dan, Jeffrey Deitch, Steven Holt and Alessandro Mendini. *Dan Friedman: Radical Modernism* (New Haven: Yale University Press, 1994).
- Hollis, Richard. *Graphic Design: a Concise History* (London: Thames & Hudson, 1994).
- Huygen, Frederique. *Wim Crouwel: Mode en Module* (Rotterdam: 010).

Coles HQ; Jasper Morrison at SCP.

Graphic Thought Facility
pp. 72–73. Science Museum exhibition designer: Casson Mann.
pp. 74–75. Product photography for Habitat catalogue (no. 3): Angela Moore.

pp. 94–95. [Two middle pictures] *Better Scenery* (mixed-media installation) by Adam Chodzko, 1999. Courtesy of Camden Art Centre, London. [bottom right] Konstantin Grcic at SCP.

2 x4
pp. 96–101. Designers: Michael Rock, Susan Sellers, Georgie Stout with Connie Purtell and Karen Hsu; Consultants: McGinty Consultants (Idie McGinty, Tim McGinty and Arden Powell).

Alexander Boxill
pp. 102–05. Photography: Andrew Penketh.

Scott King
pp. 116–21. All artwork reproduced courtesy of Magnani, London. Photography for *Crash* and *Soap Opera*: Jonathan de Villiers.

M/M
pp. 126, 128. Spring/Summer 1998, Fall/Winter 1998/1999 and

p. 153. Poster adapted from a Tristan Tzara Manifesto for Dada (1918).

Cornel Windlin
pp. 154–55. Design: Cornel Windlin and Gilles Gavillet; photography: Isabel Truniger.
p. 156. Design: Cornel Windlin and Gilles Gavillet.

Ian Wright and Bob Wilkinson
pp. 158–59. Trilogy of remix records from original material by the group Ganger: Soul 21.1 remixed by D [Darryl Moore], Soul 21.2 remixed by Two Lone Swordsmen [Andrew Weatherall and Keith Tenniswood], Soul 21.3 remixed by the

Underdog (Trevor Jackson).

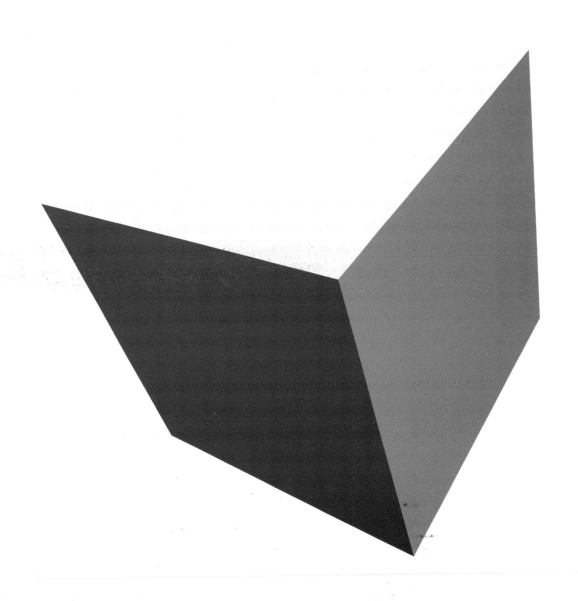